"New Women" in the Late Victorian Novel

"New Women" in the Late Victorian Novel

Lloyd Fernando

The Pennsylvania State University Press
University Park and London

Library of Congress Cataloging in Publication Data

Fernando, Lloyd.
  "New women" in the late Victorian novel.

  Includes bibliographical references and index.
    1. English fiction—19th century—History and
criticism. 2. Feminism in literature. I. Title.
PR878.W6F4   823'.8'09352   76-42456
ISBN 0-271-01241-2

for three women
Marie, Eva, Sunetra

Contents

Preface

Historical approach

This book is concerned primarily with criticism, although the chapters rely more emphatically than is customary on an awareness of social history. Browsing through the innumerable histories of the women's emancipation movement of the nineteenth century, one is particularly struck by the fact that they are histories in a conventional political kind of way. The degree of imaginative adjustment individuals were called upon to make in response to the movement remains obstinately shrouded—unless one refers to the best novelists of the period.

I therefore set out to examine whether clues supplied by social history might not assist readers in obtaining a deeper appreciation of each novelist's sensibility and a sharper perception of related critical issues. I read the history of the emancipation movement in some detail, besides rereading the novels more closely. I have also gone with much greater purpose to biographies, letters, and essays, and have frequently consulted contemporary criticism, especially contemporary reviews of the works themselves. I wanted not merely to identify in their works evidence of the authors' interest in the movement, but also to relate the evidence to the art.

The last four decades of the nineteenth century—the period covered by this book—contained a particularly tumultuous phase of the women's liberation movement which spread through many countries in Europe at the time. As it happens, this phenomenon coincides with significant changes in late Victorian fiction which it is the purpose of these essays to examine. The movement's American manifestations and their relation to the work of contemporary American novelists are not considered here, since they deserve separate study. I have concentrated on works of the great British novelists of the period partly to refute a common fallacy that their interest in the issue was marginal to their art as compared to that of their minor contemporaries. The novels have not been distorted to fit a preconceived scheme, and I have not insisted upon a stronger continuity among the chapters of this book than they obviously show. Neither do I claim that the emancipationist themes dealt with define exhaustively either the movement's potential or the developments in fiction at the time. Nevertheless, it will be seen that ideas generated by the movement, while contributing to the abandonment of older ethical values, materially affected the literary achievement of the major contemporary novelists. In other words, I have tried to indicate some important links between an influential historical movement and the development of a modern literary genre.

One might pick out W. Lyon Blease's *The Emancipation of English Women* (London, 1910) as an early example of an effort to relate English fiction to the women's movement, as it was sometimes called. *Pamela's Daughters* (London, 1937), by R. P. Utter and G. B. Needham, is more purely a history of literary taste and fashions and does not relate its interpretations to the actual condition of women in society. Of other books about women in nineteenth-century English literature in particular, Léonie Villiard's *La Femme Anglaise au XIXe Siècle* (Paris, 1920) is too brief a survey to be of much interest now; Geoffrey Wagner's *Five for Freedom: A Study of Feminism in Fiction* (London, 1972) does not include in its scope any late Victorian novel except Hardy's *Tess of the D'Urbervilles;* and Patricia Thomson's *The Victorian Heroine: A Changing Ideal 1837–1873* (London, 1956) ends about where this book begins, as does, I understand, Françoise Basch's *Relative Creatures: Victorian Women in Society and the Novel* (translated by Anthony Rudolph; New York, 1974), which I have not yet seen. In the Epilogue to this book, I refer briefly to modern liberation theorists like Germaine Greer and Kate Millett who use literary works to buttress social analysis.

It is impossible to indicate in full my indebtedness to scholarship in the field of Victorian studies. Gordon S. Haight's seven-volume edition of *The George Eliot Letters* (London, 1954–1956), a work of prodigious scholarship and imagination, greatly increased the fascination which the Victorians have held for me. For the rest I have tried to make specific debts clear through the Notes, but of course very many more scholars have contributed to my understanding of the field.

I would like to thank Professors Arnold Kettle, Michael Millgate, A. N. Jeffares, and Stanley Weintraub for early encouragement and help, and Mrs. C. Derry, E. S. Bumby, and F. Beckwith for placing at my disposal works not easily available. Professor Ron Shumaker, of Clarion State College, knows how extensively his criticisms of the

PREFACE

entire manuscript have helped me in preparing it for the press; I am truly grateful to him. I cannot adequately thank John M. Pickering, Editorial Director of The Pennsylvania State University Press, whose sustained interest and advice provided the spur for me to complete this study. Its shortcomings are mine alone. Finally, my special thanks to Marie Therese Fernando.

Acknowledgments are due to the editors of the following journals, where parts of Chapters 1, 2, 5, and 6 first appeared in different form: *A Review of English Literature, Southern Review,* and *Modern Language Review.*

L. F.

University of Malaya
Kuala Lumpur
Malaysia

Editions Used

GEORGE ELIOT: Cabinet Edition, 20 volumes (Edinburgh and London: Blackwood, 1878–1880).

GEORGE MEREDITH: Standard Edition, 15 volumes (London: Constable & Co., 1914–1920).

GEORGE MOORE: Uniform Edition, 20 volumes (London: Heinemann, 1927–1933). Complete consistency, however, is not possible. None of the three Collected Editions of Moore's works is definitive, owing to the author's repeated and, sometimes, drastic revisions. *Evelyn Innes* does not appear in any of the Collected Editions; I have used the third (revised) edition (London: Unwin, 1898).

GEORGE GISSING: Texts as published by Lawrence and Bullen, except in the cases of *The Private Papers of Henry Ryecroft* (London: Classics Book Club, 1954) and *The House of Cobwebs* (London: Constable & Co., 1907). There is no collected edition of Gissing's works.

THOMAS HARDY: Wessex Edition, 23 volumes (London: Macmillan, 1912–1913).

THE MARCH OF REFORM.

Sung at Reform Meetings in 1832; Revived at the Birmingham Jubilee Reform Meeting, 1882.

WORDS ADAPTED TO BE SUNG AT WOMEN'S SUFFRAGE MEETINGS.

By ATTWOOD.

Lo, we an-swer! See we come, Quick at Freedom's ho-ly call, We come, we come, we come, we come, To do the glor-ious work of all. And sis - ters, raise from sea to sea The sa - cred watch-word "Li - ber - ty;" And sis - ters raise from sea to sea, The sa - cred watchword "Li - ber - ty." God is our Guide, and, &c.

God is our Guide, and in His name
  From hearth, from workshop, and from loom,
We come, our ancient rights to claim,
  Those rights, with duties, to resume.
Then sisters, raise from sea to sea,
The sacred watchword " Liberty."

God is our Guide, no sword we draw,
  We kindle not war's battle fires;
By union, justice, reason, law,
  We claim the birthright of our sires.
We raise the watchword " Liberty,"
We claim our birthright to be free.

Played at the Annual Meeting of the Manchester National Society for Women's Suffrage,
Town Hall, Manchester, 1883.

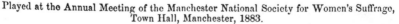

"The March of Reform." From *Women's Suffrage Journal,* 1 January 1884 (courtesy of the Manchester Public Library).

1 Novel and Ideology 1865–1895: Some Relations

The more closely one examines the idea of "women's liberation" the more complicated and nebulous it tends to become. There is an enormously varied body of literature on the subject dating from even before Mary Wollstonecraft's *Vindication of the Rights of Women* (1792), and fresh studies appear every year.[1] However the essential issues emerged with unusual clarity and force during the last thirty years of the nineteenth century in England, compelling from the society as a whole a response which deserves closer examination. What had provided a topic for occasional pamphlets since Defoe's *An Essay upon Projects* (1692) became a movement whose infiltration into ordinary lives at all levels aroused fierce partisanship as much as it challenged thoughtful consideration by others with more open minds. The literature of the period was influenced by these developments decisively enough for it to reflect the troubled adaptations which the Victorian mind was compelled to undertake. The novel, which was the pre-eminent genre, used and discarded (or demonstrated the limitations of) a series of literary techniques as it sought to encompass the human (as distinct from the theoretical or political) complexities of a social movement which demanded to be accommodated. The diversity of the responses of the best novelists of the day is what most impresses the reader. It exemplifies the prevalent artistic, social, and moral confusion into which the society as a whole was thrown. Taken as reflectors of the moral adjustments which all were called upon to make, these writers complete our understanding, built on historical and sociological studies, of the impress which the movement left upon late Victorian culture.

There was, in the first instance, the contemporary polemic concerning the place of women. The movement also focused attention on the actual legal inequities women suffered in marriage, and on the double standard of morality which stringently upheld female chastity but connived at male sexual hypocrisy. In the ensuing upheaval,

1

radical theories of a new sexual ethic were advanced—theories believed to be capable of sweeping away injustice and moral corruption at the same time, and of ushering in a completely new era in intersexual relations. A younger generation of women rather selfconsciously adopted a new life style based on such ideas, only to encounter fresh neuroses as a result. They expected sweeping changes too soon. It will be seen that by the end of the century the movement is temporarily a spent force, and that the English novel likewise reflects an exhaustion, for the time being, with searching for a point of equilibrium in relation to the movement's widest implications.

I

The polemic need not detain us long. At its root was a conflict between a profound idea of democracy expressed succinctly by T. H. Huxley in 1865 and, on the other hand, the reluctance of many opponents to believe that it could apply to women with equal force as to men. Huxley's basic principle related the demand for the liberation of women to the general notion of greater individual freedom for all. All classes of mankind, he wrote, "shall be relieved from restrictions imposed by the artifice of man and not by the necessities of Nature."[2] The liberation of women, he said, would bring "double emancipation" because "no human being can arbitrarily dominate over another without grievous damage to his own nature." Huxley's lofty dictum made little headway against long-ingrained attitudes which insisted that women, being constitutionally different, could not be accorded the same status or opportunities as men. The opposition of the traditionalists centered around three views which were labeled at the time the "domestic" theory, the "intention-of-nature" theory, and the "pedestal" theory. The first drew witless support from the view that woman's place is in the home. Frances Power Cobbe in a forceful essay entitled "The Final Cause of Woman" exasperatedly called the domestic theory "stupidly false"; John Stuart Mill, in his pamphlet *The Subjection of Women* (1869), more soberly endorsed Huxley's view by pointing to the personality damage which the domestic theory caused—"forced repression in some directions, unnatural stimulation in others."

The moot point was apparently whether nature was distorted or aided by the existing condition of women. According to the "intention-of-nature" argument, which cropped up from time to time until the end of the century, nature "intended" woman to be chiefly, even exclusively, a mother. Therefore everything which distracted her attention from this function should be treated as mischievous. A crude version of this view appeared in 1891, written by Mrs. Lynn Linton, an early sympathizer for modest feminist reforms who returned to a hard line in disgust at the later manifestations of the movement: "The *raison d'être* of a woman is maternity. For this and this alone, nature has differentiated her from man, and built her up cell by cell and organ by organ."[3] A minor novelist, Mona Caird, was stung to ask Mrs. Linton how, then, a woman's function differed from that of a cow or a sheep. Both sides, in other words, fell back on the familiar appeal to "nature," interpreting it to suit their purposes. It may not be unfair to say that on the whole the feminists were pursuing a moral point while their opponents adhered to a biological one. Although the level of public debate on this topic never rose above the mundane, we shall see in the next chapter how, in the hands of a great novelist like George Eliot, a thoroughgoing yet essentially conservative revaluation of the place of women in society grew out of the "intention-of-nature" argument and the "pedestal" theory combined, and deeply influenced one of the great novels of the English language.

The "pedestal or pinnacle theory," as the *Women's Suffrage Journal* called it, regarded woman as a minor goddess to be worshiped from afar. Probably owing something to the old code by which knights paid homage to their ladies, this attitude came to be held in Victorian times with a surprising amount of moral earnestness, as the conception of Dorothea Brooke in George Eliot's *Middlemarch* shows clearly. Frances Power Cobbe assigned particular responsibility for this tendency to Comte, who had made the deification of women an essential part of the Positivist doctrine. According to Comte, Positivism "encourages, on intellectual as well as moral grounds, full and systematic expression of the feeling of veneration for women in public as well as in private life, collectively as well as individually."[4] Women were to abstain from all practical activity, be removed from all industrial occupations, and be excluded from every kind of political activity in order that they might the better wear an aspect remote enough to seem worthy of worship. "Prayer would be of little value unless the mind could form a clear conception of its object. The worship of Woman satisfies this condition."

The acerbic Miss Cobbe questioned why women had to have their lives "regulated like those of Dalai Lamas." Women would inevitably suffer through being deprived of wholesome work, but even more through being expected to live up to an impossible ideal. Miss Cobbe then went straight to the ultimately egoistic heart of the "pedestal" theory: Comte, after all, was not thinking of women's interests, "but simply, like all the rest, he had thought, 'What can Women best do for *me?*'"[5] This comic self-contradiction in male thinking was brilliantly demonstrated in Meredith's *The Egoist* (1879). Nowadays one can easily see this novel as being among other things a merciless exposé of "male chauvinism."

John Stuart Mill took a quite different tack in rebutting the theory. With patient logic he first traced the value of "the chivalrous ideal" in the development of the human race. It flourished best, he said, in circumstances requiring individual prowess; in modern times commerce and industry had replaced fighting, and affairs were decided democratically. Therefore "a totally different ideal of morality" needed to be devised.[6] Mill offers an interesting example of a person arriving at radical feminist conclusions by systematic thinking of the utmost integrity. But he shied away from his conclusions when it came down to practical consequences. His generation (which was also the generation of George Eliot) hoped that it could adjust its attitude to women without radically altering basic traditional values. In George Eliot's *Middlemarch* (1871), discussed in the next chapter, we have a novel representing the conservative Victorian mind with brilliantly balanced truth, while Meredith in *The Egoist* (see Chapter 3) produced a great comic novel which saw primordial savagery behind apparently innocuous conventions about the second sex. These two novelists expand the rather uninspiring public debate into realms of subtlety and depth, leading their readers to ponder the significance of a movement in the role of members of human society as a whole, not partisans or opponents in a narrower struggle.

The campaign for increased educational opportunities, because it was the least controversial of feminist issues, made for that reason the best progress. The first major step in women's higher education was the founding of Girton College in 1868, under the leadership of Emily Davies. Cambridge admitted women students to the same examinations as men in 1881; Oxford followed suit in 1884. In the field of medicine women met stronger opposition, yet even here there was some progress: there were 100 women doctors in 1891. The legal profession, however, resisted the entry of women into its ranks; it nevertheless accepted a small number of women as clerks, shorthand writers, and typists. In the main, the great majority of middle-class women seeking a profession took to teaching, the number of women teachers rising from 94,229 in 1871 to 123,995 ten years later. Many others entered the public services, especially the Post Office, where by 1911 there had been "nothing short of an invasion."[7]

On the other hand, the fight for women's suffrage provoked a strong conservative reaction which gradually took the heart out of the political movement. On Mill's election to Parliament, feminists, with understandable optimism, expected immediate success. After the Reform Act of 1867, the Bill to grant women the suffrage passed its second reading by a large majority; but when it went into Committee, Gladstone, then Prime Minister, vetoed it.[8] This defeat did not interrupt the momentum the movement had just gathered. Feminists founded the *Women's Suffrage Journal* under the editorship of Lydia Becker and settled down to a determined political campaign. Between 1870 and 1880, petitions averaging 200,000 signatures were collected with the aim of promoting a Bill in Parliament. In 1880 Lydia Becker successfully innovated mass meetings of women in Manchester, London, Edinburgh, and Bristol. A revolutionary fervor gripped the movement. Feminists adopted the 1832 "March of Reform," its lyrics suitably altered, as an anthem for their meetings; in 1883 the Manchester Town Hall echoed to hundreds of women's voices singing,

> Lo, we answer! See we come
>   Quick at Freedom's holy call
> We come, we come, we come, we come
>   To do the glorious work of all.
> And sisters, raise from sea to sea,
> The sacred watchword "Liberty."
>
> God is our Guide, and in His name
>   From hearth, from workshop, and from loom,
> We come, our ancient rights to claim,
>   Those rights, with duties, to resume.
> Then Sisters, raise from sea to sea,
> The sacred watchword "Liberty."
>
> God is our Guide, no sword we draw,
>   We kindle not war's battle fires;

By union, justice, reason, law,
  We claim the birthright of our sires,
We raise the watchword "Liberty,"
We claim our birthright to be free.[9]

Dedicated canvassing at last won the support of a considerable majority of Members of Parliament. The projected Reform Bill of 1884 now held out fresh hope that women could be included in the franchise. Once again, on the brink of success, feminists met defeat at the hands of the implacable Gladstone, who threatened to withdraw the entire Bill if women were included in it. "Under the influence of this threat," the *Women's Suffrage Journal* reported sadly, "104 Liberal Members, pledged in favour of women's suffrage, voted against it when the critical occasion arose."[10] The setback confirmed many in a growing bitterness at what seemed like machiavellian tactics on the part of men, and a note of desperation crept into the movement. If women were to better their status in society they could not rely on a cooperative effort between the sexes but must fight alone.

The campaign for entry into the professions, the demand for higher education, and the suffrage movement stemmed from mainly middle- and upper-class concerns. Many feminists saw no further than these precise objectives. Even as late as 1884 we find Millicent Garrett Fawcett, a leading suffragist, declaring that they wanted the vote only "for householders in boroughs, the owners of freeholds, and the renters of land and houses, above a certain value in counties."[11] This moderation, however admirable, was maintained only by a refusal to heed the conditions in which women in the poorest classes of society lived. Since poverty drove a very large number of these women into prostitution, clandestine commerce firmly linked the two sections of society with one another. As Ray Strachey in her history of feminism observed,

> In one section of society there stood the sacred hearth and the inviolable family, and there women were, in theory, sheltered and respected, not so much for themselves as because they were the centre of the home and the guardians of the "honour" of their husbands. In the other section there were women, too, equally necessary, but very differently regarded. These women were not honoured either for themselves or for any other thing. They were exploited, bullied, and ill-treated, cooped up in the brothels of the great towns, condemned to a dreadful life

and an early death, but "tolerated," and under the "protection" of the police.[12]

Few acknowledged openly the nature of the interdependence between the two sections. Prevailing standards of propriety in England compelled even Josephine Butler against her will to exclude a discussion of it from the collection of essays which she edited, on the grounds that it was "too painful" to be treated. Nevertheless, as she wrote in her Introduction,

> *There is no analogy whatever among men, however miserable certain classes of men may be, to the wholesale destruction which goes on from year to year among women*—destruction of bodies, of consciences, of souls; and the existence of this class would alone have been enough to urge us who are happier to raise our voices to claim what we claim now—freedom and power to reach and deal with great social evils in their beginnings, and not only in a limited degree in their dire effects.[13]

At one seaport alone, Josephine Butler said, there were 9,000 prostitutes, of whom 1,500 were under fifteen years of age, 500 of these being under thirteen. Since the legal age of consent was only twelve years, the seduction of children was easy. Many such children were sold by their parents to procurers, and afterwards had little alternative but to earn a living off the streets. Young unmarried mothers in general faced this fate since the law made little or no provision for their maintenance. Ironically, the abnormally high figures for venereal disease in the Home Army—260 cases per 1,000 men—provided a telling commentary on the double standard of morality. But when the government itself, which had long connived at this state of affairs, passed penal legislation against prostitutes, it unwittingly brought matters to a head.

The story of the Contagious Diseases Acts has been repeatedly told, by no one better than Alison Neilans.[14] Alarmed at the high rate of venereal disease, the government passed preventive Acts designed to ensure that healthy women were available for the sexual gratification of its naval and military personnel. Alison Neilans details the essential crudeness of the Acts in the following terms:

> By compelling any alleged prostitute to undergo periodic examination of such a nature that if performed on any other non-consenting person it would have constituted a serious indecent assault, and placing such as were stated to be diseased

under forcible detention whereas all other venereally diseased persons were free to go about as they pleased, the State placed these women outside the protection of the common law. The danger of such legislation to other women of the poorer classes may be better imagined than described when we recall that there was no legal definition of the word "prostitute," and that any woman suspected or denounced by the "Morals Police" (i.e. a special class of police solely employed to enforce the Acts) was liable to find herself harried as a prostitute, forced to register as such, and thereafter to be regarded as a mere commodity, inspected and sold for sexual intercourse under the equivalent of a National Mark.

According to W. Lyon Blease, the most important Acts "were smuggled through Parliament in 1866 and 1869, without the knowledge of important members of the Government, almost without discussion."[15] The Acts highlighted the double standard of sex morality as it operated in Victorian society. Women forfeited their constitutional rights for an offense of which, at the very least, persons of both sexes were equally guilty. "It was as a citizen of a free country first, and as a woman secondly, that I felt impelled to come forward in defence of right," Josephine Butler said. She rallied a band of women together and published a manifesto protesting the Acts in 1869; in 1870, the year in which the *Women's Suffrage Journal* was founded, they inaugurated a journal, *The Shield,* to further their cause.

Mrs. Butler's campaign caused more embarrassment than indignation even among dedicated feminists, and left the movement divided. Women were reluctant, for reasons of strategy as well as innate shyness, to be mixed up in a public campaign which involved "endless arguments and discussions . . . on the sexual necessities of man, on the condition of brothels, and even on the details of the surgical examinations of registered prostitutes."[16] Josephine Butler therefore pursued her own course with a smaller group of supporters, but she was critical of those who approved "one part of the movement which meets their tastes or is not condemned as 'unwomanly' " and rejected the other.[17] The rawness of the subject-matter relating to the condition of working-class women received much less extensive attention from polite society as a result. An area of corruption had been uncovered, but few it seemed could bear (or dare) to analyze in full detail the ways in which it related to the whole society. W. T. Stead, the newspaper editor who dared to document the incidence of prostitution in the *Pall Mall Gazette,* was rebuffed smartly with a term of imprisonment; while Vizetelly, the publisher who launched a translation series of the works of Zola, beginning with *Au bonheur des dames* in 1883 and *Nana* in 1884, was punished in the same way. The cases of these two men assume symbolic proportions now: neither in real life nor in literature, it seemed, were the subject-matter and the methods of the French Realists acceptable on the English scene.

The conflict between frankness and prudishness in social matters finds a remarkably close parallel in the literary controversy over Realism in fiction provoked by the appearance of translations from the French Realists. By 1886 ten more novels from the *Rougon-Macquart* series had been published in England besides works by Flaubert, Edmond de Goncourt, Daudet, and Maupassant. The controversy had the curious effect of shifting, by one remove, the ground for the battle for greater frankness in literature, which one would think the English novelists themselves would have fought by example if not polemic. In actual fact the quarrel over a group of foreign authors, besides serving vicarious purposes, may possibly have aborted the full development of indigenous realists' techniques for analyzing the current revelations of squalor and injustice in Victorian society. The literary controversy invaluably supplements the social one provoked by Josephine Butler's crusade, indicating motives in the Victorian artistic and social conscience which were not completely unworthy although they remained in unresolved conflict until at least the end of the century.

Critics of the Realists opposed, in the first place, the social and aesthetic philosophy implicit in the literary method. It was deterministic, it choked off the imagination, and owing to an excessive preoccupation with fact it failed to inspire. Meredith's fiction shows how he sought to overcome this very point, that is, how he tried to marry imagination more realistically to fact, pleasant or otherwise. Their second objection, on moral grounds, was much less defensible. People were offended by the portrayal of intimate details in sex matters: the authors showed, it was said, "an almost unholy knowledge of the nature of women"; they gave rein to "filthy, libidinous propensities."[18] In vain did George Moore, in *Literature at Nurse, or Circulating Morals,* argue the right of an author to escape the tyranny of the "Young Person" who was held up as a cautionary image to those who would overstep bounds of conventional decorum. Moore's own first novel, *A Modern Lover* (1883), had fallen under the moralist critics' most potent weapon—exclusion from Mudie's circulating libraries, which meant that it went virtually unsold. Nor did Henry Vizetelly's submission, at his first trial, of extracts from Shakespeare, Defoe, Dryden, Swift, Sterne, Fielding, and Smollett, "all containing passages far more objectionable than any that can be picked out from the Zola translations published by me," make any impress either.[19] Public opinion had been reinforced by the formation of a private group called the National Vigilance Association, which campaigned for censorship, and by a House of Commons recommendation that the law against obscene publications be rigorously enforced.

We have an idea of the turmoil into which the late Victorians were thrown by both the social and literary controversies from the way individual partisans crossed lines on many of the related issues. For example, W. T. Stead was in the vanguard of the attack on Vizetelly and Zola in 1888 and 1889. Yet it was he who three years previously had made his sensational exposé, in three articles entitled "The Maiden Tribute of Babylon," detailing iniquities he had witnessed in the brothels of London—for which he too was imprisoned. Other partisans like Mrs. Lynn Linton and Mona Caird, who bitterly opposed each other on some issues, found themselves on the same side in others. If there were few heroes and heroines, there were few villains either.

Nevertheless, even though the specific tenets of Realism were not adopted by English writers except George Moore, the example of Zola, Maupassant, and others, together with the revelation of the double standard of morality in English society, had the general effect of increasing the degree of frankness in the English novel, especially in matters relating to the condition of women from the lowest classes. In this respect, George Moore's novels offer a unique challenge to both the literary critic and the social historian. He was the only writer who was directly influenced by the French Realists but he also brought other European literary trends into the English novel in an effort to portray heroines from all strata of society and not simply from the middle and upper classes. Yet as *A Mummer's Wife* (1885), *A Drama in Muslin* (1886), *Esther Waters* (1894), and *Evelyn Innes* (1898) will show, his "influences" actually fettered him artistically. Whether as Realist or as Aesthete a fundamental lack of conviction betrays him. A world view is excluded from his work, no doubt for "Realistic" reasons, while a confusion over literary methods prevents completely effective analysis in his later work. As a result his best work rests to this day in an artistic as well as social limbo which resists complete definition.

George Gissing had made a very promising beginning too under the influence of literary developments from France, but moved away, shortly after the tumultuous mid-eighties, to issues rather more than to either deterministic facts or full imagination. In the event, it was Hardy who drew out from Victorian critics, readers, and social commentators an indication of the limits of realism which they were prepared to accept. But in his hands, particularly in the 1890s, realism itself finally appeared as a method distinctively, if still uncertainly, fashioned out of native rather than foreign skills. Having labored under a tight rein from his earliest editor, Leslie Stephen, he moved from the cautious portrayal of Fanny Robin, the camp follower in *Far From the Madding Crowd* (1874), to increased boldness in the presentation of Tess and Sue Bridehead in his last two novels. It is through these later writers, then, that we can hope to obtain some inkling of the kind of psychological "brake" which the society as a whole appears to have applied on the complete exposition of the problems thrown up by the movement for the freedom of women. It would be easy to describe this response as hypocrisy or as a conspiracy of suppression; it is fairer and much more accurate to see the caution as part of a more generally instinctive though only partially successful purpose of discovering a sense of proportion with which to view deeply unsettling developments.

II

By contrast, the condition of women in relation to the permanent marriage contract received far greater attention. The pressure for reforms in matrimonial law led to a close scrutiny of the marriage relationship itself and eventually to the propounding of alternative kinds of heterosexual unions. In Chapter II of *The Subjection of Women,* John Stuart Mill presented a cogent and detailed analysis of the legal inequalities women suffered in marriage. He elaborated at length on the theme that "the wife is the actual bond-servant of her husband." She had few, if any, property or inheritance rights, nor had she legal rights to her own children; her condition was worse than even a slave's for a female slave had an admitted right "to refuse her master the last familiarity"; not so the wife. Men were not required to prove that they were fit to be trusted with the exercise of absolute power; consequently, "the vilest malefactor may have some wretched woman tied to him against whom he can commit any atrocity except killing her, and, if tolerably cautious, can do that without much danger of the legal penalty." We need not assume that these views were original to Mill—most of them in one form or another were part of the stock of arguments advanced on the subject by leading feminists of the time—but they gained immensely in coherence and prestige through being enunciated by him. Feminists campaigned strongly against such specific legal inequalities. In 1870, during Mill's term of office in Parliament, a Married Women's Property Act was passed which partly remedied the situation. Another such Act in 1882 improved the position of women further. However, Victorians came to acknowledge reluctantly the need for more sweeping reforms in law to assuage the subtle spiritual damage generated by unequal relationships which bound partners together irrevocably for the whole of their lives. It will help us to appreciate the pervasiveness of the self-examination which had now begun if we refer very briefly to a few important novels during these years.

The theme of ill-conceived or foundering marriages which emerged into such artistic prominence in the works of George Eliot, Thomas Hardy, George Moore, and Henry James may be traced, by way of historical explanation, to the searching examination, initiated by emancipationist pressure, of the real nature of the single permanent marriage bond. George Eliot's last two novels, *Middlemarch* (1871) and *Daniel Deronda* (1876), portray clear-sightedly for the first time in English fiction the jarring minutiae of marriage which raise to almost tragic levels the histories of Dorothea and Casaubon and of Gwendolen and Grandcourt. These two examples—together with the portrayal of Isabel Archer's marriage in James's *The Portrait of a Lady* (1881), of Kate Ede's in Moore's *A Mummer's Wife* (1884), and of Grace Melbury's in Hardy's *The Woodlanders* (1887)—show in different milieux virtually similar concerns on the part of their respective authors to understand and explicate the impasse which marriage as an irrevocable bond seemed of necessity to imply. In the case of George Eliot, the apocalyptic vision of *Daniel Deronda* in particular may be seen sympathetically as an effort to perceive what lay in store for women beyond the impasse. She had little to learn from the technique of realism. In the last decade of her life she moved from scrupulous, if tactful, observation to prophecy as a means of shoring up the best of an older tradition. But her younger contemporary Hardy drew more insistent attention in *The Woodlanders* to the waywardness of the sexual impulse (through Fitzpiers), highlighting thereby a permanently vitiating factor in the lifelong bond.

To return: few Victorians could bring themselves to believe in divorce as a constructive solution to the problem of failed marriages. John Stuart Mill himself steered away from the problem. *The Subjection of Women,* we may sometimes forget, was principally a political pamphlet; it aimed to marshall support for feminine emancipation, and it succeeded in this aim to a considerable degree. But it is quite clear that, partly for reasons of strategy, Mill stopped deliberately short of tracing the moral implications of his argument to their furthest conclusion. The following passage indicates a crucial gap in *The Subjection of Women:*

> Surely, if a woman is denied any lot in life but that of being the personal body-servant of a despot, and is dependent for everything upon the chance of finding one who may be disposed to make a favourite of her instead of merely a drudge, it is a very cruel aggravation of her fate that she should be allowed to try this chance only once. The natural sequel and corollary from this state of things would be, that since her all in life depends upon obtaining a good master, she should be allowed to change again and again until she finds one. I am not saying that she ought to be allowed this privilege. That is a totally different consideration. The question of divorce, in the sense of involving liberty of remarriage, is one into which it is foreign to my purpose to enter.

Mill's refusal to deal with this problem (although he has shown it to be logically implied by feminist claims for equal treatment) reveals how even progressive opinion looked on the related topics of divorce and remarriage as quicksands endangering the entire structure of sexual ethics at the time.

Reforms in law progressed with infinite slowness. The Matrimonial Causes Act of 1857 had transferred jurisdiction over marriage disputes from Church courts to a new civil court. This Act did not place the two parties on an equal footing—adultery gave the husband the right to a divorce, but not the wife, except in cases of incest, criminal prosecution, or extreme cruelty. The stringency applied even to legal separation, which the wife could obtain only under special conditions and at great expense, since the tribunal was fixed in London. In effect, "Divorce was reserved for the rich and the inhabitants of London and the home counties," not for the suitor from remote districts.[20] Hardy's *The Woodlanders* offers an illustration of this particular point in Melbury's abortive trip to London to seek a divorce for his daughter Grace (Chs. 37–39). A few small but useful concessions were prized out of Parliament after great difficulty. Minor Acts passed in 1878, 1886, and 1895 made some provision for women as the injured party, in respect of the legal custody of her children, and maintenance for herself.[21]

These small gains on the one hand indicate how relations between men and women were now under unprecedented scrutiny, but also suggest the strength of deeply ingrained traditional attitudes, with which feminist leaders had to contend, towards the position of women in marriage. It is no wonder that they and their followers concentrated, on the whole, on less controversial matters. If we glance at the major novelists once again, we find that Meredith alone took a positive approach to divorce and remarriage as feasible solutions. In *Diana of the Crossways* (1885) and *One of Our Conquerors* (1891) he tried by means of a cryptic rhetoric to exorcise the nebulous feelings of moral guilt besetting men and women marrying a second time. In part, the idiosyncratic qualities of Meredith's style may be related to his tacit acknowledgment of the immense difficulties in the way of bringing about a major revolution in law and convention. Yet the tide was not to be stemmed. A kind of underground extremist theory had been building up from as far back as the 1850s, and radical views on the problems raised by the movement—of sex, divorce and remarriage, and free love—won a currency in inverse proportion to parliamentary and conventional intransigence.

III

"It is the complete disregard of sexualogical [sic] difficulties which renders so superficial and unconvincing much of the talk which proceeds from the 'Woman's Rights' platform," Karl Pearson wrote. Pearson, a socialist university lecturer, published two papers—"The Woman's Question" (1885) and "Socialism and Sex" (1887)—whose radical views influenced a new generation of young women in the eighties.[22] Pearson owed much to the cool rational daring of an earlier theorist and medical practitioner, G. R. Drysdale, but it is helpful to deal with Pearson's views first because, chronologically, Pearson made the more immediate impact while Drysdale's blunter

14

and even more far-reaching ideas penetrated and seemed to remain at subconscious or unspoken levels of thought. Both men shifted the ideology of the movement above the level of partisan struggle and related it to versions of a totally new society.

Pearson believed that "the two most important movements of our era are without doubt the socialistic movement and the movement for the complete emancipation of women." In his paper "The Woman's Question" in 1885 he argued that women's liberation would entail "a revolutionary change in social habits and sexual ideals." What is more, he pointed out that the perfect total and legal equality of men and women would be accompanied by "the entire reconstruction of the family, if not of the state." He dismissed as absurd the view of woman's proper place as being in the home, since it failed to take account of the twenty per cent of women who remained single.

Pearson held that the emancipated woman was entitled to knowledge—would indeed seek it—and, "because of the social responsibilities her emancipation must bring," that meant sexual knowledge as well, something completely excluded by existing taboos. He said, "Men and women are not only surprisingly ignorant of each other's thought and phases of feeling, but extremely often, of each other's constitution; nay, not only of each other's, but occasionally of their own." Obviously, the Victorian ideal of purity based on this kind of ignorance helped no one. On the other hand, sexual knowledge would also encourage sexual freedom for women. Would this eliminate the double standard of morality which had been displayed in so blatant a fashion by the passing of the Contagious Diseases Acts? In the existing state of affairs, both men and women were subject to the law of monogamous marriage, but, through society's connivance at prostitution, only men were permitted sexual freedom. Pearson inclined to think that corresponding sexual freedom for women would eradicate prostitution since it seemed likely "that our social system, quite as much as man's supposed needs, keeps prostitution alive." Therefore, though he took care to avoid being dogmatic, he asserted, "Sex-equality must either be marked by the cessation of prostitution among men, or if it remains, the like freedom to women."

In "Socialism and Sex," which he wrote two years later, Pearson examined the consequences of his thinking in the context of a socialist society, because, in his view, the socialist and the feminist "are essentially fighting the same battle." Economic independence under socialism would enable a woman to preserve her moral dignity and complete freedom of action. In bearing a child, a woman would suffer some limitation of freedom and the state would help preserve her economic independence by contributing to her maintenance and that of her child. State interference was further justified on account of the need to preserve "the limit of efficient population." Only under these conditions would the goal of complete emancipation be a reality: the free woman would then be able to form or break her sex-relationships independently. "Legalised life-long monogamy" would be superseded by a relationship based on *"pure affection, raised above every suspicion of constraint, and every taint of commercialism"* (author's italics). Pearson argued, "It is not a question of sensuality or sexual experiment, but of indomitable law. Variations are taking place in our views and actions with regard to sex, which are but forerunners of the new type" of moral code. The following extract summarizes the essence of his views:

> I hold that the sex-relationship, both as to form and substance, ought to be a pure question of taste, a simple matter of agreement between the man and [the woman], in which neither society nor the state would have any need or right to interfere. The economic independence of both man and woman would render it a relation solely of mutual sympathy and affection; its form and duration would vary according to the feelings and wants of individuals. This free sexual union seems to me the ideal of the future, the outcome of socialism as applied to sex.

Pearson did not envisage general promiscuity as a result of his proposals; indeed, for all the radical nature of his views, he still seems to have maintained a belief in an ideal of marriage differing from the legalized institution only in the absence of conventional and religious sanctions. "The men and women who, being absolutely free, would choose more than one [lover], would certainly be the exceptions—exceptions, I believe, infinitely more rare than under our present legalised monogamy." Everything depended on women's good sense to ensure that "the equality of the sexes will not again connote the return of a swamp-age such as befell the tottering Roman Empire." Such an eventuality, if it did occur, would call for drastic measures including "a second subjection of one sex" to restore social stability. These reasoned views by a university lecturer held progressive feminists spellbound with excitement, while horrifying their opponents. Pearson, however, on his own admission had "only touched the veriest fringe of a vast subject"—though he sketched the essential implications of a movement whose significance even many feminists underestimated. The issue of women's liberation did not concern women alone. Much that men had taken for granted would be swept aside, if the principle of women's independence was conceded.

On the whole question of sexual emancipation, G. R. Drysdale was one of the few writers in Victorian times to get to the very nub in insisting plainly that sexual satisfaction was essential for the physical and moral well-being of both the individual and society. His book, *The Elements of Social Science, or Physical, Sexual and Natural Religion,* was dedicated to the proposition that "The ennoblement of the body in ourselves and in others is just as high an aim for man as that of the spirit."[23] It originally appeared in 1854 and was republished almost annually for half a century, reaching its twenty-fifth edition in 1886—Pearson's essays, as we have seen, appeared in 1885 and 1887—and its thirty-fifth in 1905.

Drysdale, a doctor of medicine, discussed poverty, Malthusianism, prostitution, and female emancipation with unsurpassed frankness, drawing them together in a radical ethic which few societies officially countenance even today. Malthus had pointed out that since increases in population directly aggravated social poverty, sexual abstinence was the only means of averting economic misery. Contradicting this, Drysdale said that sexual abstinence was too great an evil to use as a remedy. He went even further and declared, *"The ignorance of the necessity of sexual intercourse to the health and virtue of both man and woman, is the most fundamental error in medical and moral philosophy"* (author's italics).

Drysdale deliberately made no distinction between sexual intercourse and love; one was the other. Young married men could palliate their need for love by "degraded and clandestine" means: they had recourse to prostitutes; but the want of love was acutely felt "by no class so much as by young ladies." The author gave a figure of 1,407,225 women between the ages for twenty and forty years who never married. In their case sexual abstinence accounted for "the universal prevalence of hysteria, menstrual disease and . . . other evils." Thus the existing code did not allow men and women to lead good and virtuous lives.

Marriage was no solution: its irrevocable nature and the impossibility of procuring divorce led to "the most fearful evils." In a single paragraph, Drysdale put the emancipationist case against marriage:

Marriage is one of the chief instruments in the degradation of women. It perpetuates the old inveterate error, that it is the province of the female sex to depend upon man for support, and to attend merely to household cares, and the rearing of children—a belief which is utterly incompatible with the freedom of dignified development of woman on the one hand, and with the economical interests of society on the other. It is the emblem too of all those harsh and unjust views, which have given to woman so much fewer privileges in love than man, and have punished so much more severely a breach of the moral code in her case. For a man to indulge his sexual appetites illegitimately, either before or after the marriage vow, is thought venial; but for a woman to do so, is the most heinous crime. The wife has been held, in the true spirit of the oriental harem, to be in a manner the sexual *property* of the husband, whom no one had a right to touch, and who had no right to have a thought for anyone but her own lord and master. (author's italics)

Since the rigor of the prevailing sexual code did not prevent an immense amount of unmarried intercourse, Drysdale literally urged his readers to make a virtue of the prevailing violation of the code. He proposed as the first principle that "every individual should make it his conscientious aim, that he or she should have a sufficiency of love to satisfy the sexual demands of his nature, and that others round him should have the same." He was advocating a far wider concept of free love than Karl Pearson did. In striving for a higher state of sexual morality, Drysdale said, it was absolutely necessary "that other modes of sexual intercourse [than that in marriage] be considered honourable and legitimate. If a man and woman conceive a passion for each other, they should be morally entitled to indulge it, without bringing themselves together for life." Considerateness and a sense of responsibility would prevent abuse of this permissiveness. "We should endeavour to act in an open and dignified manner towards those with whom we have any sexual relations; and never to deceive them." A couple should not have children without being prepared to rear them. By such means, prostitution would be eliminated and society would secure the abatement of needless suffering due to unwarranted moral coercion. Since Drysdale devoted some space to contraceptive intercourse and at least a third of his book to the symptoms and treatment of venereal diseases, he cannot be said to have had his head in the clouds in proposing his radical ethic. He was nevertheless an idealist, almost a visionary, who saw in "the universal distribution of the pleasures of love" the cure for many of society's ills, including the subjection of women.

Drysdale was never mentioned by name by emancipation theorists, not even by Pearson, whom, we may assume, he directly influenced. Pearson differed from Drysdale in being far more wary of general promiscuity; Pearson also interpreted free love as a social theory, where Drysdale held it to be a fundamental individual need not necessarily tied to a union of some duration. Crucial as these two distinctions are, it was nevertheless plain that both writers envisaged far-reaching structural and legislative changes in society after women had been fully emancipated. Principally, the long-dominant patriarchal system was threatened, the laws of inheritance and illegitimacy would be revolutionized, and the concept of the family as the basic social unit would be greatly modified. Although, officially, feminists shrank from discussing such prospects, a new generation of young women in the eighties was elated by the thought that their movement involved so much. "The power of the book [Pearson's *The Ethic of Free Thought*] lies in its stimulating quality," wrote Olive Schreiner.[24] Spurred by the views of Pearson and Drysdale, numbers of young women, with a kind of selfconscious determination, began to put some of the more radical feminist ideals of equality and independence into practice in their own lives.

IV

Olive Schreiner's letters give us some idea of the psychological and emotional make-up of these progressive women. "Our first duty is to develop ourselves," she wrote. "Then you are ready for any kind of work that comes. The woman who does this is doing more to do away with prostitution and the inequalities between man and woman, and to make possible a nobler race of human beings, than by all the talking and vituperation possible. It is not against men we have to fight but against *ourselves* within ourselves."[25] From Olive Schreiner's example, we gather that the "New Woman" adopted a rather naive, but still refreshingly honest, approach towards matters of sex, marriage, and love. Olive Schreiner confided to Havelock Ellis that during her menstrual periods "my feelings are particularly sensitive and strong," and she enjoined him to be similarly observant about "the interaction of your manly upon your mental nature" for she wished to know "the man's side of the question."[26] The search for fresh absolutes of conduct now mattered more to her than heeding the traditional taboos decreed for women by convention, and she accepted her role as pioneer with a sense of responsibility and even of humility. She said, "One cannot hasten sight; it has to grow clear slowly. When one breaks away from all old moorings, and shapes a higher path of morality for oneself, and perhaps for others who shall follow one, it cannot be done without suffering."[27]

The "New Woman" held no brief for promiscuity, that is, for indiscriminate sexual intercourse. Nor, at first, did she appear to entertain seriously the prospect of forming new unions if earlier ones proved unsuccessful. In rejecting conventional marriage, she was rejecting the religious and social forms, the deadwood, to which society attached greater importance than to love. For her "free love" meant the restoration of priorities. Where love bound equals, there true marriage was, and she took it for granted that the love should—or would—be a lifelong thing. In *The Story of an African Farm* (1883), Olive Schreiner's heroine, Lyndall, might say to her suitor, "I cannot marry you because I cannot be tied; but if you wish you may take me away with you, and take care of me; then when we do not love any more we can say goodbye" (Pt. 2, Ch. 9), but in actual life the author adhered to the view that

> The one and only ideal is the perfect mental and physical life-long union of one man with one woman. That is the only thing which for highly developed intellectual natures can consolidate marriage. All short of this is more or less a failure, and no legal marriage can make a relationship other than impure in which there isn't this union. How we should arrange that this great pure form of marriage may be oftenest and most perfectly reached seems to me a great problem.[28]

We note in passing that this view is not remarkably different from the definition of "Free Love" given in the *Encyclopedia of the Social Sciences*.

However, the realization, which came to be acknowledged especially in the nineties, that not even the free union could assure permanence brought to the fore more difficult issues which "George Egerton," Mrs. Golding Bright by her third marriage, developed with some artistic skill. Her two volumes of short stories, *Keynotes*

(1892) and *Discords* (1894), evoke a genuine though fleeting sense of the moral and emotional complexities implied by countenancing successive free unions. Whether she portrayed a divorcee seeking a truer emotional basis in a second marriage, as in "A Little Grey Glove," or whether she depicted the free woman who would courageously accept a man's love for only so long as he was prepared to give it, as in the "The Regeneration of Two," the author was able to suggest, at least, the great resources of moral stamina needed to form and dissolve human relationships and re-form new ones.

The conduct and frank opinions and writings of young women like Olive Schreiner, her friend Eleanor Marx (daughter of Karl Marx), and George Egerton struck English society as a new and daring phenomenon. Owing to the threat they presented to long-established values and conventions, these young pioneers became targets of wrath in two stern articles in the *Nineteenth Century*. Their author, Mrs. Lynn Linton, ignoring the intense and often quite touching idealism of most emancipated women, labeled them "Wild Women" and strongly chastised them for "warring as they do against the best traditions, the holiest functions, and the sweetest qualities of their sex."[29] Her attack, which in many ways marks the hardening of the opposition to the ideology of the movement in its later stages, did no more, however, than vehemently restate some of the familiar objections to the liberation of women.

The division in women's ranks had already been indicated publicly two years earlier, in 1889, when one hundred women including Mrs. Humphry Ward, Mrs. Leslie Stephen, and Mrs. Matthew Arnold appended their signatures to an article opposing female suffrage as well. Alarmed at the emergence of a more radical generation of feminists, they asserted "that the emancipating process has now reached the limits fixed by the physical constitution of women and by the fundamental difference which must always exist between their main occupations and those of men."[30] Although suffragists came back swiftly with an effective reply to which more than two thousand signatures were appended, opponents of the movement had regained the initiative and were to gain full ascendancy in the mid-nineties. The novels of Gissing reflect the alarm of such opponents at the undeniable shoddiness that had crept into the society—not solely attributable, of course, to the feminist movement. Originally attracted to the French Realists, Gissing had followed their manner in writing an excellent early novel, *The Unclassed* (1884), but his subsequent writing was increasingly based on mere polemic against the movement. The reasoned animosity present in his later fiction, especially, permits us to evaluate the conservative reaction to sweeping change, while throwing sharper light on factors which prevented his rising to full artistic power.

The "New Woman" had not only to run the gauntlet of strong criticism; she faced rather more insidious defeat within her own psyche, in the form of numerous and persisting ailments which she did not fully understand. In a letter to Havelock Ellis, Olive Schreiner mentioned some of the curiously similar complaints from which she and her friends suffered:

> The pain in my stomach that I used to get when I had to eat before people was really asthma in the stomach, caused by the terrible excitement of my heart from nervousness and misery. I have an interesting letter from that Miss A. P.—[sic] I told you of who suffered even more than I did. She has described *all* I suffered. A—[sic], you know, also suffered in the same way, and Eleanor Marx, I know, did. I am writing to ask her about it; I think she will speak frankly of it. But now here comes an interesting fact. A— P—'s sister is the most terrible sufferer from asthma that I ever saw in Europe and Eleanor's sister, Jenny, suffered from her earliest childhood till the day of her death from asthma. I think I have often told you of the curious relation I found between that convulsive feeling in the stomach and the asthma. I will send you all the letters I get from women about it.[31]

It was easy enough to pour scorn on the pioneering efforts of these women: the strain of initiating new criteria of behavior exacted a heavy personal toll in the form of neuroses. Some were driven to rancor against men, and others to extravagance in conduct; from the example of the extramarital union of Eleanor Marx and Edward Aveling, they realized bitterly that an ungenerous male could easily take advantage of their naively idealistic approach to the issue of women's independence.[32] A few out of ungovernable hatred for the male hypocrisy revealed by the episode of the Contagious Diseases Acts, and also perhaps out of repugnance for sexual relations instilled by prudish upbringing, totally repudiated all contact with men.[33] These latter were the extremist radical feminists who directly inspired the smouldering lesbian characters of Cecilia Cullen in George Moore's *A Drama in Muslin,* and of Olive Chancellor in Henry James's *The Bostonians,* both of which appeared in 1886. George Moore described such extreme feminists as

22

women who in the tumult of their aspirations, and their passionate yearnings towards the new ideal, and the memory of
the abasement their sex have been in the past, and are still
being in the present, subjected to, forget the immutability of
the laws of life, and with virulent virtue and protest condemn
love—that is to say love in the sense of sexual intercourse—
and proclaim a higher mission for woman than to be the
mother of men. (*A Drama in Muslin,* Bk. 2, Ch. 4)

Naturally the warping of human nature which excessive fervor for
emancipation had wrought in some "New Women" offered excellent
material for the novelist—and for the dramatist also, as Strindberg's
and Ibsen's plays show. There may, however, be some danger of
assuming too readily that the sexual aversion bordering on pathology
which Moore and James portrayed was peculiarly symptomatic of the
female temperament alone, or at any rate, of women with extreme
emancipationist ideals. In point of fact, the aversion was found in
both sexes.

By now, Victorians could avoid no longer the conclusion that the
challenge of the movement for the freedom of women had become
at last a challenge on sexual issues, for it induced, more than any
other movement did, a fresh consciousness and acknowledgment of
individual sexual motivation in human relationships. They were
unable to fit this discovery into their traditional scheme of value, and
thus found themselves saddled with the seemingly unresolvable, and
therefore morally disconcerting, dualism in love which had plagued
Christian societies for many centuries.[34] We can only guess at the
degree of repugnance which Victorians felt at being forcibly confronted anew by a tarnished ideal. Some people, according to Karl
Pearson, advanced the view "that man's sexual instincts have been so
abnormally developed that they have become a disease." Others,
including a few extreme feminists, appear to have looked forward to
an ultimately sexless state. On the whole, Victorians found this latter
prospect even more depressing than present sexuality. Nevertheless,
in its physical aspect, love reminded them of their kinship with
animals, a stage from which they fervently hoped they were evolving
away. Love in the end would be wholly spiritual; meanwhile the
physical aspect was accepted on sufferance.

That the "New Woman" acknowledged the physical at all (albeit
theoretically) was sufficient to outrage conservative sensibilities; yet
she shared in the fundamental emphasis of the age in regarding the

physical as simply an uncongenial complement to the mental, possibly eradicable in ideal circumstances. In a letter to W. T. Stead, Olive Schreiner defined this characteristic attitude:

> To me it appears that in a highly developed and intellectual people, the mental and spiritual union is more important, more truly the *marriage,* than the physical. I should feel it (and I think any person who has reached a certain stage of growth) a much more right and important reason for terminating a union, that the person to whom I was united had fuller, deeper and more useful mental union with another than that there should be a physical relation. Just the mental union, "for the begetting of great works," to me constitutes marriage. Of course there are millions, even in the most civilized communities, for whom physical attraction, affection and fidelity must constitute marriage. But for natures more highly developed I believe such a union to be wrong. Continuance of the physical relation when the higher mental relation is not possible, and when the affection is given elsewhere, seems to me a more terrible because a more permanent prostitution than that of the streets.[35]

As the century moved to its close, the failure of the Victorians to achieve a satisfactory synthesis of the dual aspects of love filled them with revulsion for all who reminded them of their dilemma. The "New Women," who may not all have been fully aware of the complexity and scope of the wider issues which the ideology of the movement raised, bore the brunt of this reaction, despite a plea that their conduct "partakes of the frailty of human nature, and ought not to prejudice a really impartial mind against the views themselves."[36]

Their views had been more and more openly expressed in novels with heroines more and more openly defiant. In the final decade of the century the theme of free unions especially had become widespread, though without once producing an outstanding work. Many problem-novelists, enamored of the "advanced" implications of the women's movement, rapidly sacrificed the artistic potential of the novel as a literary form for the sake of illustrating particular views or theses on such topics as woman's role in society, the double standard of morality, and free love. The attitude of these minor authors and their heroines was basically what D. H. Lawrence was later to label "sex in the head." Hardly anyone apart from Hardy acknowledged the irrational hiatus which sexual feeling brought into unions. He had deferred to editorial censorship long enough. With his reputation as a novelist well established, he finally gave the problem-novelists an object lesson in their field with the publication of *Jude the Obscure*. This novel held up to the public a frank reflection of unacknowledged neuroses caused by new life styles, and made evident the serious divisive implications of a movement which had begun thirty years previously with a fine zeal. It provoked a vehemence which signaled the end of the movement's most influential phase.

The movement had bade fair to overthrow more than it actually did. By 1895 the Contagious Diseases Acts had been repealed and women had begun to be admitted into institutions of higher education and into some of the professions. But the call for women's suffrage failed repeatedly, and reforms in the marriage laws bore little relation to the magnitude of some of the problems exposed by thirty years of agitation. Although the militant phase of the suffrage campaign was still to come, the urgent sense of general radical challenge which the movement evoked in these years was never recaptured. The "New Women" learned the familiar, sad lesson that establishing the justice of ideals was only the first step—a comparatively simple one—in setting a social process in motion. The more difficult and unpredictable task was to assimilate into one's own personality the consequences of one's vision in a hostile or uncomprehending society. The hardest task of all was to cause that vision to pass insensibly into society so that the substance of its habits and manners, its way of seeing, might be significantly changed. As for the development of the English novel we have only to observe a startling contrast to appreciate with what remarkable closeness the movement and the literary form existed during those years: compare the wonderfully discriminated body of life in *Middlemarch*, which stands at the beginning of this stirring period, with the fevered and fragmented representation of a confused new generation in *Jude the Obscure* at the end of it. We shall study the stages of this phenomenon in the chapters that follow.

2 George Eliot: "Emotional Intellect" in a Widening Ethic

When issues relating to the freedom of women came to the fore in the late 1860s, George Eliot maintained toward the movement a considered aloofness which puzzled many of her friends. The year 1866, in which the first of the notorious Contagious Diseases Acts was passed by Parliament, also marked the publication of *Felix Holt,* her sixth novel. She was famous now, with throngs of fervent admirers, while her private life had more or less ceased to be an embarrassment. It had been a long and difficult road back. Twelve years previously her "open defiance of the marriage convention" had been undertaken with a complex mixture of rational thought and passionate emotion.[1] Religious scruples had not been at issue; nor, at the other extreme, was the then thirty-five-year-old Marian Evans about to espouse the cause of indiscriminate sexual liberty. "Light and easily broken ties are what I neither desire theoretically nor could live for practically," she told Mrs. Charles Bray.[2] Yet her association with George Henry Lewes, perhaps the most famous free union of the period, was emblematic of the new radicalism just beginning. In Lewes's marriage to Agnes Jervis she had perceived the irrelevance, the cruelty even, of upholding a legal tie where substance had been completely destroyed. Since Lewes could get no relief from the rigid law governing divorce, George Eliot found in the depth of their attachment for each other ample justification for ignoring the law.

Inevitably her mature response to a difficult situation provoked misunderstanding even among her close friends, let alone members of the general public. It was to take her years of patient private correspondence to convince those for whose opinion she cared of the essential rightness of what both she and Lewes regarded "as a sacred bond" (*Letters,* II, 349). However, her brother Isaac Evans remained unreconciled to her until her death. She sought to persuade others who took exception to the match to concede at least that "it is possible for two people to hold different opinions on

26

momentous subjects with equal sincerity" (*Letters,* II, 213–215). For herself she took this principle a stage further, upholding the validity of her stand not in exclusiveness but in a dynamic relation with that of others who subscribed to the ethical principles of the day. To put it simply, while by her action she had engaged in a major assault on orthodox ethics, she retained the profoundest respect and compassionate understanding for continuity despite inevitable change.

George Eliot's personal rebellion was successful because she never relaxed the wholeheartedness with which she tried to relate her own life to the best values of her society. Of course her works played their part too in earning, besides wide acclaim, a readier sympathy for her position. The novels, from *Scenes of Clerical Life* in 1857 to *Felix Holt* in 1866, convinced readers that a new, great novelist had emerged. This growing reputation considerably assisted her and Lewes over long years in making their peace with English society without prejudice to their union. While, however, she was never to forget "the peculiarities of [her] own lot" in discussing women's issues, reformers of various kinds could not understand why she did not plunge into the fray with greater zest (*Letters,* IV, 364). She seems to have had her doubts even on the advisability of giving women the vote, writing to Sara Hennell to "scold" her "for undertaking to canvass on the Woman's Suffrage question." She asked, "Why should you burthen yourself in that way, for an extremely doubtful good?" (*Letters,* IV, 390). Preoccupation with the public moves required too many simplifications which she was not prepared to concede. In general she seems, therefore, to have been content to let those with decided opinions have the political field to themselves. Her attitude to John Stuart Mill was precisely and scrupulously just, no more. She did not consider that his logical and democratic approach to the subject had much bearing on her own, and she had to discourage the inclination on the part of one or two of her correspondents to couple, automatically, Mill's views with hers. To Mrs. Peter Taylor she wrote, "On the whole I am inclined to hope for much good from the serious presentation of women's claims before Parliament" (*Letters,* IV, 366). The carefully guarded approval in principle is clear, as is also the implicit reservation of her right to a separate opinion on specific measures.

Letters which George Eliot wrote, especially in the sixties, have a remarkable bearing on women's issues. Her views outline a theory of the sensibility, based on interaction between emotion and intellect, which went beyond specific issues of the day. The theory attempts to place women's best aspirations in relation to the heritage of the past, the problems of the present, and the hopes for the future. In her novels she progressively developed it in a way which elevated the claims of women for equal status with men to the level of a literary theme capable of inspiring the highest art. It is instructive to begin by examining the nature of the distinction between the sexes which she sought to make. Dealing with "the physical and physiological differences between women and men," she wrote, in a letter to Emily Davies,

> On the one hand these may be said to lie on the surface and be palpable to every impartial person with common sense who looks at a large assembly made up of both sexes. But on the other hand the differences are deep roots of psychological development, and their influences can be fully traced by careful well-instructed thought. Apart from the question of sex, and only for the sake of illuminating it, take the mode in which some comparatively external physical characteristics such as quality of skin, or relative muscular power among boys, will enter into the determination of ultimate nature, the *proportion* of feeling and all mental action, in the given individual. This is the deepest and subtlest sort of education that life gives. (*Letters,* IV, 467, author's italics)

Her argument is scientific after the fashion of nineteenth-century thinkers. Woman's "ultimate nature" is different from man's in this essential: it possesses, or is capable of, a higher proportion of feeling. Under this category are apparently included such emotions as "love, pity, constituting sympathy, and generous joy with regard to the lot of our fellowmen."[3] The naturalistic basis of the distinction is emphasized by George Eliot's firm association of this capacity of woman with her sexual function—what she calls discreetly "the other primary difference"—which gives her "that exquisite type of gentleness, tenderness, possible maternity suffusing a woman's being with affectionateness, which makes what we mean by the feminine character" (*Letters,* IV, 467). Woman's sexual function may put her at a disadvantage, biologically speaking, "but for that very reason I would the more contend that in the moral evolution we have 'an art which does not mind nature'" (*Letters,* IV, 364). So far George Eliot insists chiefly that women are different from men—not, as one might think, such an obvious distinction if we bear in mind the tendency of some feminists to confuse equality with similarity. She justifies the value of that difference by attributing to it a moral power: "It is the function of love in the largest sense to mitigate the harshness of all fatalities" (*Letters,* IV, 364). This may sound as if woman is being relegated once more to her traditional role of comforter: the woman will comfort the man in his struggle with "the pressure of hard non-moral outward conditions" (*Letters,* IV, 365). Yet there are numerous hints in the letters that she meant something much more, namely, an epistemological function which feeling performs.

The evidence allows, admittedly, only a tentative reconstruction of that function, and in the succeeding sections of this chapter we shall have to look to the novels to fill it out. How do we know and understand the nature of the world in order to live successfully in it? Largely, George Eliot argues, through fearless rational thinking—"to *fear* the examination of any proposition appears an intellectual and moral palsy"—and through the "firm grasping" of substantial nature (*Life,* I, 106, author's italics). These propose an affirmation of the concrete world which she readily endorses but finds incomplete. The knowledge which the scientific study of material phenomena yields is useful but fragmented. The scientific approach does not restore, once it has divided the world into fields of study for analysis, the original, functional, living unity. These deficiencies should not therefore lead us away to emotional epicureanism at the other end of the scale. The truest perception of the unity of life becomes possible only when feeling, irrational and irreducible, suffuses scientific study. Then we have "an experience and knowledge over and above the swing of atoms" (*Letters,* VI, 99). Feeling is the necessary complement equally on the individual and on the universal plane. It is its integrating capacity—"constituting sympathy"—that gives it importance, high moral value (*Life,* III, 48).

Thus there are two equally important, complementary modes of perception: intellect which probes, and nonanalyzable feeling which integrates. It is in their marriage—"emotion blending with thought"— that the truest knowledge for living is obtained, for this is the fundamental principle of the life process (*Letters,* VI, 124). It operates at every level and scale, moving from the unit to the mass, from the specific to the general, since the behavior of each unit has an influence on the ultimate behavior of the mass. "The progress of the world," George Eliot wrote, " . . . can certainly never come at all save by the modified action of the individual human beings who compose the world" (*Letters,* VI, 99). The process begins with the individual, who has to achieve a blend of the two kinds of perception which will lead to the complete realization of his possibilities of growth and development. When a man marries a woman he allies himself still further with the natural life process, since while both are endowed with intellectual capacity the essential difference between them lies in the woman's capacity for a higher "proportion of feeling." Lifelong marriage is not a mere social convention; its justification is affirmed on fundamental grounds. "Human love, the mutual subjection of soul between a man and a woman . . . [is] a growth and revelation beginning before all history," she wrote (*Letters*, IV, 467). "The possibility of a constantly growing blessedness in marriage is to me the very basis of good in our mortal life" (*Letters*, VI, 117).

George Eliot makes some nice distinctions. Woman is not all feeling; she herself must seek a marriage of the two kinds of perception within her. "We women are always in danger of living too exclusively in the affections; and though our affections are perhaps the best gifts we have, we ought also to have our share of the more independent life—some joy in things for their own sake" (*Letters*, IV, 467). She goes on to develop this idea and indicts women's education: "All their teaching has been, that they can only delight in study of any kind for the sake of a personal love. They have never contemplated an independent delight in ideas as an experience which they could confess without being laughed at." The independent delight in ideas serves, also, purposes beyond the individual. It makes for the ideal marriage which in its turn "enters into the perfection of life" (*Letters*, IV, 467). But while remaining convinced that women ought to have the same access to knowledge as men, George Eliot did not believe that their interests and pursuits should be exactly similar, or that women should seek to mold their personalities on the male pattern (*Letters*, V, 58). That would efface the distinctions in "woman's peculiar constitution" and undermine her capacity for the "special moral influence" in the progress of the world (*Letters*, IV, 467).

These views about woman's nature and her place in society may appear to have a coherence suggesting something like a system. In actual fact George Eliot was aware of the difficulties of setting out clearly a conception of woman's place of such a magnitude. She was reluctant "to undertake any . . . specific enunciation of doctrine on a question so entangled as the 'Woman Question'" (*Letters*, II, 396). The furthest reaches of her thought were, in fact, well-nigh inexpressible; her ideas were simply too large to be set forth in expository prose. The chief characteristic of her thinking is that it is drenched in evolutionary implications. Though the theory of evolution originated in studies in the natural sciences, it is, for her, universally applicable. Metamorphoses which occur in every branch of life and every kind of human aspiration are only stages "in the working out of higher possibilities," the "Promethean effort" toward which is made through feeling (*Letters,* IV, 472). Religion evolves as does society; the human race will continue to develop on principles discovered in nature.

Women by virtue of their sex can play an important role in the progress of the human race, since they are by nature endowed with a larger capacity for feeling, which has been discovered to be intellectually and morally valuable. The endowment is not unique to their sex; the difference is one of proportion. Nor are all women equally so endowed; there are, naturally, individual differences. Each woman, if allowed to nurture her real potential, herself changes for the better in the process, and makes a contribution which influences the development of the race. George Eliot wrote,

> The one conviction on the matter which I hold with some tenacity is, that through all transitions the goal towards which we are proceeding is a more clearly discerned distinction of function (allowing always for exceptional cases of individual organisation) with as near an approach to equivalence of good for women and for men as can be secured by the effort of growing moral force to lighten the pressure of hard non-moral outward conditions. (*Letters,* IV, 364)

No contemporary feminist platform, not even Mill's pamphlet, contained ideas as large as these. The best traditional values of love, charity, and compassion have been taken out of the context of specific Christian dogma and reworked thoroughly in terms of the new knowledge of science and human development. An emphatic secularism is thereby introduced, supported by intellectual and scientific premises. It rescues the concept of tradition from a position of arrest and makes it dynamically subject to change. It defines this process as consisting in large measure of an infinitely varying concatenation of circumstances beyond human power to control but yet offering modest opportunities for human choice. That choice is moral; its manifestation in action is through feeling. Women are thus given an unprecedented role in human life, complementary not subservient to that of men. Yet the overall conservatism of this system cannot be denied. George Eliot's vision of humanity, according to a contemporary reviewer, was of a river wending its way down a channel whose direction is now hardly alterable.[4] The scope for human intervention, while of the highest importance, is also tragically limited. There will be no revolution. There will only be a gradual changing of the sensibility of the race as a whole, resulting from the accumulated efforts of individual human beings.[5]

It is in her novels that George Eliot gives dramatic and lifelike validity to her radical, abstruse thinking on the place of women in relation to an evolving concept of the human sensibility. In *The Mill on the Floss* (1860), *Middlemarch* (1871), and *Daniel Deronda* (1876), for instance, George Eliot demonstrated how ineluctable was the reality of "hard non-moral outward conditions," meaning, one suspects, the power of the forces of conservatism, besides deterministic circumstance. In this intricate web she perceived her heroines Maggie, Dorothea, and Gwendolen striving for the fullest realization of their potential—which involved, essentially, making crucial moral choices in matters of feeling. They had to learn to employ "emotional intellect," as she eventually called it, "as if it were a faculty, like vision" (*Daniel Deronda*, Chs. 41, 36). Here she posed for herself an artistic challenge of great magnitude, one that she did not overcome with complete success—that of fusing the stories of her vital heroines into the whole stream of life. The village of St. Ogg's becomes the province of Middlemarch which in turn gives way to an international context in *Daniel Deronda,* in which "a binding theory of the human race" is sought. Similarly, Maggie is succeeded by Dorothea, who belongs to the middle class, followed by Gwendolen, who would play the haughty beauty of international society. These heroines exemplify an emotional yearning and power disproportionate in realistic terms to their worlds but, artistically speaking, highly successfully drawn. Henry James recognized the almost uncanny attractiveness of the women in George Eliot's novels. Considering Dorothea Brooke, he found himself wondering how she came to be so strikingly represented:

> To render the expression of a soul requires a cunning hand; but we seem to look straight into the unfathomable eyes of the beautiful spirit of Dorothea Brooke. She exhales a sort of aroma of spiritual sweetness, and we believe in her as in a woman we might providentially meet some fine day when we should find ourselves doubting of the immortality of the soul. By what unerring mechanism this effect is produced—whether by fine strokes or broad ones, by description or by narration, we can hardly say; it is certainly the great achievement of the book.[6]

Although Maggie and Gwendolen do not quite come up to this degree of spiritual refinement, they are, with Dorothea, varying renditions of a basic portrait of a woman of high spirit who finds her most eager aspirations toward knowledge, life, and love thwarted or at best severely controlled. But while the author's female portraiture increased in power, beauty, and dramatic intensity, the creative dichotomy between the women and their worlds, always a challenge demanding resolution by the novelist, had become with the appearance of *Daniel Deronda* a finally catastrophic division leaving the older Victorian novel itself, like the society which it closely reflected, broken in twain. *two*

I

The comprehensive vision of the *The Mill on the Floss* (1860) and the flaws arising from the incomplete relation of minute detail to width of design confirm that with this work the author made her first strenuous effort to examine present problems in the context of past wisdom. She is less interested in advocating practical improvements in the condition of women than in facing the challenge that moral independence for women entails striking changes in traditional ethical values. As if to ensure that this function would not be missed by readers, a wealth of authorial commentary accompanies the narrative, drawing attention to larger principles of value behind apparently mundane events. With this novel George Eliot embarked on a search, which was to occupy her for the remainder of her life, for an ideal balance between the art of the novelist and the response of a woman committed to the problems of her day. The art of the novelist, everyone agrees, prevails admirably in the first two volumes of *The Mill on the Floss*. The unhurried accumulation of human detail conveys an indelible sense of the solid, prosaic lives of the Tullivers and Dodsons. Swinburne was led to rhapsodize on "the first two-thirds of the book" as "perhaps the very noblest of tragic as well as of humorous prose idylls in the language."[7] But when we come to the third volume we find, with the *Westminster Review,* that "the groundwork of fact disappears, and the problem of Maggie's nature alone occupies the author's attention."[8] George Eliot herself conceded this when she spoke of "a want of proportionate fullness in the treatment of the third [volume], which I shall always regret" (*Letters,* III, 317).

We must be careful not to insist on a wider structural hiatus than is actually there. Important episodes in Maggie's adult life are unobtrusively foreshadowed in the period of her childhood, a method which binds to some extent the novel's uneven parts. A "half-hidden symbolism," noted by the *Spectator,* organizes its central ideas.[9] The current of the river Floss parallels the current of life, tradition, and society in St. Ogg's. Both are "deaf and loving" (Bk. I, Ch. 1), and both will overwhelm Maggie. These adjectives highlight the ambivalence with which the author skilfully creates Maggie's world. They indicate a precisely balanced regard for the forces of conservatism. Mr. Tulliver's loss of the water rights carries with it the discreetest suggestion that the authority to speak for tradition itself is not necessarily permanently vested in one source but is, rather, open to debate. The Tullivers and Dodsons, taken as a group, exhibit pettiness, narrowness, and paganism, despite their inherited Christian beliefs.[10] Tom represents the continuing Tulliver and Dodson tradition, exerting over Maggie an authority which is as deaf and loving as the river that will eventually destroy them both. Maggie herself is the chief medium through whom the novel advances the concept of an evolving ethical system "to correspond with a widening psychology" (*Letters,* III, 318). She represents feeling, aspiration, and the impulse to "[rise] above the mental level of the generation before [her]" (Bk. IV, Ch. 1). Maggie rebels against the settled assumptions of her milieu even as she concedes the irrevocability of her bond with it, symbolized in her abiding love for Tom. She is not outside the stream of life but very much within it.

Maggie is as much an individually realized character as an idea. The key incidents of her life have a decided bearing on the fact of her sex. She is "too 'cute for a woman," her father observes. She has read, even as a little girl, Defoe, Jeremy Taylor, and Bunyan. She attempts to deny her sex by cutting off her hair, because of the preconceived notions her elders hold concerning the nature of women and their secondary status in society. She pushes Lucy Deane, society's own ideal well-brought-up woman, into the mud, and she even attempts flight (to the gypsies). The latter two episodes are echoed grimly enough in her later career. Through her flight with Stephen she pushes Lucy Deane again into the mud, metaphorically speaking, and as from the gypsies, so from her elopement she returns with the realization that her individuality and aspirations must somehow be adjusted to a context which cannot be escaped.

The treatment of Maggie's search for emotional balance between exercising one's freedom and maintaining a continuity from the past shows how the novel, in George Eliot's hands, has broken bounds defined by her major predecessors, Jane Austen and Charlotte Brontë, both in scope and in moral concerns.[11] Jane Austen shaped trivialities of thought, speech, and conduct into exquisitely designed plots highlighting personal moral crises. George Eliot adds to these elements the "hard non-moral outward conditions" of the material world. When the bailiffs are in Tulliver's house and his furniture is cleared away by his creditors, we have a kind of crisis different from the kind which concerned Jane Austen. George Eliot's crises alert one not only to the individual dilemma but, at graduated levels, to the dilemmas of a class of persons, and relate both individual and class to the impersonal movement of life. Charlotte Brontë might deal more frankly than in the past with the complexities of Rochester's love for Jane Eyre, but Jane's problem is sterilized to a significant degree. For one thing, as Joan Bennett has pointed out, "there is no one connected either with [Rochester] or with Jane who can be injured by their union."[12] For another, there is little danger that Jane herself will deviate from inherited principles. Jane resolves, "I will keep the law given by God; sanctioned by man. . . . Preconceived opinions, foregone determinations, are all I have at this hour to stand by me: there I plant my foot."[13] In Maggie Tulliver's world there is no such neatness, nor such security.

Maggie has fled with Stephen, who is betrothed to Lucy, her friend. She has broken faith with Lucy, and violated a social canon through her elopement. She is thus brought to confront the dilemma which the exercise of complete freedom of action raises for responsible individuals. The difficulty in resolving the dilemma, Maggie finds, is that religious sanctions carry no conviction any more—"there was no flavour in them—no strength" (Bk. IV, Ch. 3); departures from the social law, even when undertaken with integrity, bring "false imputations" (Bk. VII, Ch. 2); and judgment, on which alone the independent person can rely, finds "no master key that will fit all cases" (Bk. VII, Ch. 2).

Essentially Maggie's society compels her to choose one, and only one, of two alternatives. Either she can choose to maintain her ties with her family and with established social values, or she must be prepared to give them up completely if she chooses instead to minister to her desires for a fully realized love and for the fulfillment of her yearnings for a wider life. As one critic puts it, her tragedy arises from "having to choose between goals that are equally good but incompatible."[14] In the first case, her independent growth and development will end; in plain terms, feeling will be sacrificed to duty. Thomas à Kempis's teaching on renunciation which has powerfully moved her—"lay the axe to the root, that thou mayst pluck up and destroy that hidden inordinate inclination to thyself" (Bk. IV, Ch. 3)—must be implemented. For Maggie this means that Stephen must be given up, and the truth of the passion of love denied, so that she may retain her original place in society. If she chooses the second alternative, preserving her right to independent moral action, she will be breaking away completely from her milieu. Maggie recoils from this alternative (which is not simply rebellion against society but an early example of the concept of alienation) almost by instinct, and for the right reasons. As she tells Dr. Kenn, "I have no heart to begin a strange life again. I should have no stay. I should feel like a lonely wanderer—cut off from the past" (Bk. VII, Ch. 2). The twentieth-century idea of the outsider, living a life completely apart from her fellow human beings, does not enter into her head at all, even as it has no place whatsoever in her author's own philosophy. Maggie is not a potential Merseult. Even as a wanderer Maggie would try to "begin a new life, in which she would have to rouse herself to receive new impressions" (Bk. VII, Ch. 5). Wherever she might be she must build, build a new complex of relations, even though it would hardly compensate for the loss of "the past."

Maggie is too intelligent to accept these mutually exclusive alternatives as a complete summation of her problem. Her "emotional intellect" urges her to seek out a way in which they may be brought into a more moderate relation with each other so that her yearnings for love, knowledge, and equality may interact creatively with the established values of her society. Maggie's odyssey works up to this climax from her early childhood, namely, the challenge to resolve "the great problem of the shifting relation between passion and duty" (Bk. VII, Ch. 2), or between individual independence and tradition. She has a glimpse of a truth to which, in the author's words, "eyes and hearts are too often fatally sealed—the truth that moral judgements must remain false and hollow, unless they are checked and enlightened by a perpetual reference to the special circumstances that mark the individual lot."

Maggie does not recoil from this individually worked-out third prospect to whose verge she has inexorably moved. She simply withdraws from it in despair, knowing that her society is not ready to countenance pioneers for a widening ethic. She decides not to marry

Stephen, saying, "I cannot take a good for myself that has been wrung out of their [Lucy's and Philip's] misery" (Bk. VI, Ch. 14). She is also ready to face social opprobrium by returning to St. Ogg's to "atone in some way to Lucy—to others, . . . [to] convince them that I am sorry" (Bk. VII, Ch. 2). It would appear that she therefore chooses the first alternative, that of placing duty before passion. But her submission is not true repentance. It recalls, rather, that voluntary "stupefaction" of the moral sense of which Philip Wakem had warned her. He had said,

> "It is stupefaction to remain in ignorance—to shut up all the avenues by which the life of your fellow-men might become known to you. I am not resigned: I am not sure that life is long enough to learn that lesson. *You* are not resigned: you are only trying to stupefy yourself." (Bk. V, Ch. 3, author's italics)

Maggie knows that it is her quailing before the prospect of great, fresh, moral exertions and not any basic unsoundness in her yearnings which has contributed to her defeat. She chooses to accept the judgment of St. Ogg's while remaining secretly unconvinced that she is guilty of any fundamental wrong. Almost the last words she utters are, "I will bear it, and bear it till death. . . . But how long it will be before death comes! I am so young, so healthy. How shall I have patience and strength? Am I to struggle and fall and repent again?" (Bk. VII, Ch. 5). By this time the unattractiveness of ethical and social mores which have remained closed to considered change has also been exposed. Their manifestations in the ironic portrayal of the Tullivers and Dodsons and especially in Tom's final inflexibility leave one in no doubt on this score. More fundamentally, the inviolability of the past has also been subtly eroded when we consider what has happened to Thomas à Kempis's teaching on renunciation: it is not wholly distinguishable any more from "stupefaction." Dr. Kenn is half led to believe, after all, in "the idea of an ultimate marriage between Stephen and Maggie as the least evil" (Bk. Vii, Ch. 2). Maggie's plight makes renunciation seem like mere propitiation to household gods, a wasteful deference to "oppressive narrowness" (Bk. IV, Ch. 1), rather than a doctrine that has been triumphantly vindicated.

The success of *The Mill on the Floss* in demonstrating the unavoidability of the trend towards "a widening psychology" and with it a widening ethical system may be gauged from the outraged responses of critics of its own day. Swinburne was apoplectic in his reaction to the part of the novel dealing with Maggie's flight with Stephen, calling it a "flagrant blemish . . . a cancer in the very bosom, a gangrene in the very flesh . . . [only] removable by amputation and remediable by cautery."[15] In more restrained fashion the *Saturday Review* found a Lawrentian streak in George Eliot's treatment of love "as a strange overmastering force which, through the senses, captivates and enthrals the soul."[16] Such views confirm that readers were troubled both by the truthful representation of the passion of love in serious English fiction and by the undermining of the traditional view of a permanent and unchangeable sexual ethic. It may not have been entirely a coincidence that it took a woman reviewer to perceive that the presentation of Maggie's dilemma was a commentary on the restrictions governing women at the time. Dinah Mulock asked what future there was for "the hundreds of clever girls, born of uncongenial parents, hemmed in with unsympathizing kindred of the Dodson sort, blest with no lover on whom to bestow their strong affections."[17] More importantly, Mulock realized that with this novel the opening salvoes in a coming revolution in morality had been fired: "there is a picturesque piteousness which somehow confuses one's sense of right and wrong."

Yet it is only when one examines the nature of the symbolic contending forces in this novel that one is able to understand just where the author's controlling design has gone askew. George Eliot has boldly matched, on equal terms, Maggie's aspirations with the imperceptible movement of life in St. Ogg's. The emphasis on Maggie as one of two major counterbalancing elements in the novel, whatever its technical demerits, is an indication of the extent to which the author was prepared to go to plead that women were as capable of high yearnings as men and as "liable to great error" (*Letters,* III, 318). In recent years critics have hardly attended to the resulting structural lopsidedness, preferring to concentrate on the emotional lopsidedness in the portrayal of this character. The criticism that "in George Eliot's presentment of Maggie there is an element of self-idealization" identifies only a small part of the problem, besides depending too exclusively on speculation about the author's personal psychology.[18] That George Eliot drew on her personal experience to an unascertainable extent in depicting Maggie need not be denied—all good authors do. She has also depicted the fundamentals of the moral problem she herself personally faced when she decided to live with Lewes. But the partisanship in the portrayal of this character may with greater aptness be explained as a partisanship for her sex. It is more interesting to examine the novel's flaws on these terms than in relation to the author's so-called immaturity.

In pitting Maggie as the representative of her sex against her wider environment George Eliot rested her novel on a fallacy. She was not writing a prose *Antigone* depicting the conflict between personified authority and the individual (Creon versus Antigone) but rather the conflict, so it would seem, between the movement of life and the individual. There is something uncomfortable and inapt in this opposition. George Eliot's thinking depended for its power on the subtlest distinctions between feeling and intellect. In *The Mill on the Floss,* if Maggie represents feeling, and the world of the Tullivers and Dodsons, against which she is matched, represents the slow movement of life, no one of comparable forcefulness stands for intellect. The crippled Philip Wakem, the intellectually and emotionally inferior Stephen Guest, and even the "preternaturally hard" Tom Tulliver (as the *Westminster Review* described him[19]) offer little on the same scale to match Maggie's dominant role.

Furthermore, the kind of feeling Maggie represents is too personalized and does not reverberate to any main current of human sensibility such that it can support a binding theory about the sexes together, such as we have seen implied in the *Letters.* This does not mean that George Eliot was indulging her own daydreams. She merely sought to objectify her concept in a single character, which is a good way to begin making an abstract concept fictionally plausible. As she herself probably realized, this first approach was a failure so far as any wide design for the novel as a whole was intended. The portrait of Maggie is drawn completely in realistic terms, a method which does not allow, with impunity, excessive rhetorical emphasis and certainly not lengthy nebulous thinking on the part of any character. One guesses that this might be why, when the author went on to depict Dorothea Brooke in *Middlemarch,* she added a frankly persuasive element in characterizing her, a controlled breakout from purely realistic confines, so as to affiliate Dorothea to past religious and artistic ideals. Yet even the undeniable success of this experiment in *Middlemarch* apparently did not satisfy George Eliot. Feeling had to be dramatized even more extensively to reveal its furthest reaches not just through women but as a beneficent impulse behind entire historical movements of the present and future. The discussion of *Daniel Deronda* in the final section of this chapter will show how, more clearly than elsewhere, this last novel offers a complete anatomy of feeling which George Eliot sought to represent in her fiction, while revealing the inability of the genre itself to bear a persuasive function of that magnitude on behalf of it.

In an important way, *The Mill on the Floss* is the author's most daring assault on prevailing mores, but it leaves the free woman at an impasse. There is enough to suggest that George Eliot could have gone further, but the effort in the novel's closing pages is too rushed for us to be certain. One notes, however, that it is not only Maggie who is drowned but Tom too. The rudimentary symbolism suggests that her whole problem itself will be swept away. If Maggie is given her deserts, St. Ogg's is inundated by the flood too. The movement of life is greater than either. As the novel stands, that is a veiled suggestion rather than a fully realized idea.

II

A survey of the criticism of *Middlemarch* from the time of its first appearance to the present day shows that while a feminist theme has been detected in the novel its importance has been generally discounted. A contemporary review in *The Times* noted that "A certain school may think that Dorothea's story involves some special impeachment of the present female lot," and commented:

> We do not think this is at all intended, and if it be intended it is certainly not justified. George Eliot gives us a noble portrait and an affecting history of a woman who nearly spoilt her life by attempting to rise above her opportunities, but her failures and mistakes are not due to the fact of her being a woman, but are simply those which belong to the common lot of human life.[20]

The issue has been reconsidered recently by Barbara Hardy, who makes a number of interesting points about "the *ex officio* disability of being women" shared by most of George Eliot's heroines, including Dorothea Brooke. For example, they are uneducated, and find few opportunities for employment, factors which may drive them "into a passive and tormenting ennui like Maggie and Gwendolen," or into unsuccessful marriage like Dorothea. Barbara Hardy's conclusion, however, is similar to that of *The Times*:

> Any suggestion of a feminist moral is controlled and extended by the complex plot, which puts Dorothea in her place as an

example less of a feminine problem than of the frustrations of the human condition.[21]

This verdict does not do justice to the way in which George Eliot's complex understanding of the feminist issue lent a profound bias to her conception of Dorothea Brooke. When we also consider that Dorothea's own fortunes highlight the problem of marital incompatibility we are led to discover unsuspected depths of organization in the entire novel which, while maintaining its own inner logic, was also governed by a deeply felt response to the movement for women's freedom.

Earlier in this chapter, grounds were set out for believing that the characterization of Dorothea was directly inspired by George Eliot's highly intellectual conception of the place of women in the scheme of things. Dorothea is intended to represent an impressive conception of mid-Victorian womanhood cramped by restrictions placed upon her by society. There is an undeniable persuasive element in her portrait which it would be futile to try to "resolve" by realistic standards alone. It was probably this element which led to James's remark that Dorothea "is of more consequence than the action of which she is the nominal centre."[22]

Dorothea's spiritual and cultural genealogy is affirmed with a confidence that is breathtaking: she is a modern Saint Theresa with the presence of the Blessed Virgin, the latter a comparison which Lydgate explicitly makes. In the crisis in which loss of reputation, insolvency, and marital unhappiness are all intertwined, he has been to see her and comes away thinking, "This young creature has a heart large enough for the Virgin Mary" (Ch. 76). Naumann, with a painter's eye for essentials, ecstatically declares, "Here stands beauty in its breathing life, with the consciousness of Christian centuries in its bosom" (Ch. 19). One gathers she is in the mainstream of a scheme of spiritual aspiration evolving beyond doctrinal religion. It is not necessary to deny that this ambitious affiliation of such an attractive heroine with a spiritual pantheon through the ages constitutes a piece of special pleading by the author on behalf of her sex at a time when questions about the nature of woman were being vehemently discussed. W. J. Harvey suggests that a saving irony operates.[23] No doubt it does; but the religious perspective confirms the scope in which the character was conceived which, in numerous little touches, gives the early chapters of *Middlemarch* their compelling power.

Since religion is subject to evolution as much as any other factor in human life, the impulse in past ages to venerate a Blessed Virgin was not inherently wrong; it merely had not found its proper human object, which was the exalted quality of womanhood. By means of an extraordinary feat of imagination George Eliot imbues Comte's view of woman with a semblance of moral truth. The degree to which Comtean ideas influenced the author in the writing of *Middlemarch* has been discussed recently, but the way in which the portrayal of Dorothea relates to these ideas has not been clarified.[24] In its larger dimensions the character illustrates Comte's concept of successive historical stages through which religion, theology, and metaphysics evolve toward a modern, positive outlook. We can see this particularly in the ways in which the great enlargement of the portrait retains credible contact with the character in her more mundane preoccupations.

Like her creator, Dorothea has come to have no interest in the doctrinal or devotional aspects of religion; in the crises of her life she does not pray.[25] She has gone beyond theistic belief to a stage which she entreats Ladislaw not to call "by any name" (Ch. 39). Dorothea's responses are at once impulsive and categorical; sometimes they are determined in advance, as when she decides to accept Casaubon before he has proposed to her (Ch. 3), or when hearing of the blight which Lydgate has come under through his association with Bulstrode, she "energetically" exclaims, "Let us find out the truth and clear him!" (Ch. 71). Under the "coercion" (Ch. 3) of her essential qualities she expresses herself with a spontaneity which Middlemarch society regards as extreme. Her behavior does not conform to the accepted conventions regarding the well-brought-up young woman. She is not satisfied with the only two avenues open to her: charitable activity or marriage. The questions "What could she do, what ought she to do?" (Ch. 3) give a Positivist bias to her restlessness (besides a feminist one of which she is oblivious), impelling her to seek a role for her strong, unused energies. Opinions of Dorothea in Middlemarch society range from Mr. Bulstrode's "not my style of woman" (Ch. 10), through Celia's bourgeois exhortation to Dorothea to "listen to what James says else you will be getting into a scrape" (Ch. 72), to Mr. Chichely's "altogether a mistake, and calculated to shock his trust in final causes" (Ch. 10). Dorothea challenges them all by marrying a man twenty-seven years older than herself, and a pillar of their static world. She is thus personally plunged into a dramatic situation which will test the validity of her emotional power.

In joining the story of the large-souled "Miss Brooke" to the novel of Middlemarch society, George Eliot removed from the scene the heroine to whom she had devoted ten full chapters and introduced the remaining principals in the next eight (Chs. 11–18). But when she returns to Dorothea in Rome (Chs. 19–22), the attempt to make a virtue of necessity is not wholly successful. Authorial reticence in one direction (the failure of the marriage) vies unevenly with expansiveness in another (the relation of Dorothea's plight to the classical heritage of Rome). That Casaubon is impotent and that the marriage in all probability has not been consummated are details which have been judiciously teased out by Barbara Hardy.[26] There is a kind of magic-lantern projection of this breakdown against the ruins of Rome with its "vast wreck of ambitious ideals, sensuous and spiritual" (Ch. 22). It is not surprising that there is strain here, even a slight incoherence since the attempt is to compress into a few pages an ambitious art-history perspective for the heroine, besides her spiritual one.

A piquant irony does partially save these pages, particularly where Dorothea serves as a model for a painting: the portrait of another defeated protagonist of the human spirit is added to history's wrecked ideals by—further irony—Naumann, "one of the chief renovators of Christian art" (Ch. 22). Ironic representation is further advanced in Naumann's artifice of using Casaubon as model for his painting of Saint Thomas Aquinas "sitting among the doctors of the Church in a disputation too abstract to be represented." The heir of Aquinas with his influential metaphysics is Casaubon, "elaborator of small explanations" (Ch. 21). We recognize the irony but must admit that contrivance is to the fore, and that special pleading, in the form of exaggerated female portraiture, has here produced undue rhetorical emphasis. There is nevertheless an attempt to make this emphasis dramatically plausible. "All this immense expense of art . . . seems somehow to lie outside life and make it no better for the world," Dorothea says (Ch. 22). Brought up short by the prospect of lifelong marital incompatibility, she is able to distinguish the more acutely between her own "vigorous enthusiasm" (Ch. 19) and Ladislaw's shallower romanticism. Ladislaw's artistic ideal is divorced from present reality, a relishing, according to Pater, of beautiful feelings for their own sake. Dorothea's great positive force stems from her desire, clarified under the pressure of her own marriage, to employ the artistic impulse directly in the problems of life. The nature of art itself is changing because it is life itself which must be made beautiful.

43

Dorothea's foil, of course, is Rosamond Vincy, every Middle-marcher's ideal woman. In portraying her, George Eliot subjected the convention of the well-brought-up young lady to close scrutiny, and R. H. Hutton confirms that the point was taken by contemporary readers:

> This exquisitely painted figure is the deadliest blow at the common assumption that limitation in both heart and brain is a desirable thing for a woman, that has ever been struck.[27]

Where the spirit of Dorothea's spiritual and cultural forebears burns unquenched in her, Rosamond is conscious of her actual forebears only, and with shame. She wishes she "had not been the daughter of a Middlemarch manufacturer" and does not want to be reminded "that her mother's father had been an inkeeper" (Ch. 11). She fits with ease into the mold decreed for her. She shows no "unbecoming knowledge" (Ch. 27), while no one exceeds her in matters like "propriety of speech" and "musical execution" (Ch. 11). She is the best product of "the chief school in the county" (Ch. 11). The gentlemen show a monotonous uniformity in their appreciation of these qualities. "I like a woman who lays herself out a little more [than Dorothea] to please us," says Mr. Bulstrode (Ch. 10); "I like them blond, with a certain gait, and a swan neck," says Mr. Chichely (Ch. 10); Lydgate feels sure that "if he ever married, his wife would have . . . that distinctive womanhood which must be classed with flowers and music" (Ch. 16). A woman should have nothing to do with anything so vulgar as the actual problems of living. Her virtue is her remoteness from life so that she can the better charm away a man's cares.

In Rosamond this trivializing of her nature transforms her, by an inexorable logic, into a force of destruction instead. In the Lydgate-Rosamond marriage, master and plaything exchange roles: it is the master who is manipulated with the deadly skills of the studied response. The role which society wants Rosamond to play becomes second nature. After her marriage she flirts with Ladislaw at the same time as she embarks upon another flirtation with Lydgate's cousin. Having no inner conviction in the worth of maintaining any personal relationship, she is eventually assailed by the kind of malaise which Ibsen was to dramatize brilliantly in the character of Hedda Gabler:

> She was oppressed by ennui, and by that dissatisfaction which in women's minds is continually turning into a trivial jealousy, referring to no real claims, springing from no deeper passion

than the vague exactingness of egoism, and yet capable of impelling action as well as speech. "There is really nothing to care for much," said poor Rosamond inwardly. (Ch. 59)

If Rosamond is Dorothea's foil, Lydgate is her match. Although Dorothea and Lydgate have been very frequently compared and contrasted in critical discussions, no one has examined the fundamental reasons for considering them as a pair at all. Lydgate is even regarded as not being as important a character as Dorothea, which is surprising since he is the chief character of the second of the two books which were eventually conflated to form *Middlemarch*. By considering the two characters in the context of the revaluation of the relationship between the sexes, one can bring to light neglected aspects of their relationship to each other—or as some would prefer to put it, their very lack of a living relationship with each other. We have not yet given full weight to James's observation concerning them in his famous review: "The mind passes from one to the other with that supreme sense of the vastness and variety of human life, under aspects apparently similar, which it belongs only to the greatest novels to produce." To put it bluntly, we have not contrasted these two in sexual terms, believing it, one supposes, to be uncalled for. An inordinate amount of critical attention has been devoted instead to Dorothea's relationship with Ladislaw.

In defining the basis on which her relationship with Lydgate should attract prior attention, W. J. Harvey's elucidation of Lydgate's intellectual interests is helpful.[28] Lydgate sees the medical profession as holding out the promise of "the most perfect interchange between science and art" (Ch. 15). That there is a degree of error in the basic hypothesis behind his projected research does "place" him, as Harvey shows, but there is enough in the quality of his thought still to make him a worthy counterpart to Dorothea. There is an "arts/science-syndrome" air about the way the two complement each other, and it is tempting to argue that Lydgate, not Ladislaw, is Dorothea's soul-mate. But how, one may ask, do their careers substantiate this? We have seen that George Eliot's "philosophy of life" rested on the sense of the continuity of tradition modified by individual moral choices. Every endeavor had to be devoted to promoting success in marriage, for the advancement of life itself depended upon it. On the other hand, the histories of Dorothea's marriage and Lydgate's show an incisive awareness of the prevalence of marital incompatibility.

45

There are two disadvantages in accepting the fable at the heart of *Middlemarch* as that of a rescue into love, as Barbara Hardy proposes.[29] First, we are compelled to give fuller weight than is necessary to the end result of that rescue, the falsely romantic association of Dorothea and Ladislaw—with the consequent dissatisfaction we have not been able to exorcise for years now. Second and rather more seriously, we underestimate one of the gripping successes of the major part of *Middlemarch,* the impressively authentic, and artistic, representation of marital incompatibility, Dorothea's and Lydgate's with their respective partners. After the conflation of the two separate writing projects George Eliot had embarked upon, *Middlemarch* was no more the story of "Miss Brooke" alone but of Lydgate as well—he holds the center of the other half of the novel. Since the novel appeared at a time when the relations between the sexes, particularly in marriage, were under searching scrutiny, it is difficult to ignore this external resonance of the drama of their failed marriages. One does not wish to claim any particular artistic merit for *Middlemarch* simply because it does analyze the disturbing reality which was the subject of so much contemporary controversy; rather it is that the controversy alerts us to an unsuspected basis for comparing Dorothea with Lydgate, and thereby further defines the core of the novel's art.

Do we not sometimes unconsciously subscribe to the conventional myth that there are such things as ideal pairs? Dorothea and Lydgate fit that myth remarkably well. It is a moot point how far George Eliot had the ironical intention of enticing the reader to speculate on the course their lives would have taken had they married. Dorothea appeals to Lydgate before any other character for advice in her distress in marriage (Ch. 30). Exigencies of the plot in the first place—Casaubon's first attack—have brought Lydgate to Lowick, but there is a play on the parallels and differences of their natures suggested through their "vocations," Dorothea being to Saint Theresa as Lydgate is to Vesalius. The force of the analogy does not stop here. The pair also represent the sexes in a fundamental way. Dorothea's turn to help Lydgate in his own defeat comes at the end of the novel when his marriage and career are near ruin. They are kindred natures, not in being similar, but in the status of each as the nearest ideal complement of the other. Dorothea recognizes this fact instinctively; Lydgate's awareness grows on him with each successive meeting; and the reader is stirred by this speculative attraction of contraries. At the same time it is true, as the novel stands, that their sense of kinship is not simply sexual attraction but a more inclusive, "Promethean" kind (*Life,* III, 48).

The novel's artistry is distinctively served, then, by keeping them, maritally speaking, apart. Their largely separate fortunes constitute a major ironic metaphor emphasizing what for the author was the most pernicious "non-moral" fact of all: that true integration of feeling and intellect has to be sought in a stream of life so incredibly complex as to preclude worthwhile success before we even begin. An ideally successful marriage almost never comes about. In terms of George Eliot's deterministic philosophy the essential tragedy lay here. The movement of life in the mass does not, of its nature, adapt itself to the true potential of this or that particular element within it. The irony lies in the fact that meetings are rarely opportune, and in the further teasing ambiguity—creatively generated by the novel's way of showing how small circumstances go to make or unmake large events—concerning whether Lydgate and Dorothea would in fact have made a successful marriage if they had met when still uncommitted. It is the open-ended nature of the contrast between the two which is fascinating. The largely separate paths on which these two characters are set even before they meet symbolize the fundamental divergence plaguing the successful marrying of the sexes.

But what of the marriages which do take place? How do they extend the analysis of the relations between the sexes, and further define the pattern of character relationships in the novel? A remarkably similar rhetoric is used in portraying the courtships of Casaubon and Lydgate, with an almost identical ironic aim. Lydgate, engaged to Rosamond,

> felt as if already breathed upon by exquisite wedded affection such as would be bestowed by an accomplished creature who venerated his high musings and momentous labours and would never interfere with them; who would create order in the home and accounts with still magic, yet keep her fingers ready to touch the lute and transform life into romance at any moment; who was instructed to the true womanly limit and not a hair's breadth beyond—docile, therefore, and ready to carry out behests which came from beyond that limit. (Ch. 36)

Casaubon's expectations of happiness proceed, not surprisingly, at a sedate pace but are not different in kind from Lydgate's more ebullient imaginings. Key phrases in his letter of proposal to Dorothea (Ch. 5) strikingly echo Lydgate's thoughts in the passage above.

Casaubon's labors are "grave," Lydgate's "momentous"; Casaubon expects that Dorothea will "cast a charm over vacant hours," Lydgate that Rosamond will "transform life into romance at any moment"; Dorothea is expected to "supply" Casaubon's needs, Rosamond must be "ready to carry out [Lydgate's] behests." Casaubon's hopes are only an older and more tired version of Lydgate's. We are told that Casaubon took a wife "to adorn the remaining quadrant of his course, and be a little moon that would hardly cause a calculable perturbation" (Ch. 11), and the satellite metaphor aptly underlines the conventional myth about relations between men and women which both men share, as did their contemporaries. The strokes of characterization even here have a resonance beyond the individual.

Characteristically, George Eliot goes to the source from which the myths about love and marriage spring. Discussing Casaubon's courtship, she comments, "We all of us, grave or light, get our thoughts entangled in metaphors, and act fatally on the strength of them" (Ch. 10). Certain modes of expression, if relied upon uncritically, impose characteristic kinds of conduct and ideals which bear little relation to the realities of the marriage partnership. For Casaubon marriage is hardly more than "an outward requirement, and [he] was bent on fulfilling unimpeachably all requirements" (Ch. 29). Lydgate is no different: "he was no radical in relation to anything but medical reform and the prosecution of discovery"; for the rest "he walked by hereditary habit" (Ch. 36). Both men are heavily paternal toward their wives, expecting submissiveness as of right. Casaubon finds Dorothea "not qualified to discriminate" (Ch. 37), and Lydgate angrily asks Rosamond to "learn to take my judgement" (Ch. 58). The convention of male intellectual and moral superiority being rigidly upheld, the expected promise does not ensue.

The crisis in each marriage consists essentially of the downfall of the man from his self-assumed position of lord, contributor to the world's knowledge, and guardian—in a way that goes near the bone. "And all your notes," cries Dorothea, "all those rows of volumes— will you not now do what you used to speak of?—will you not make up your mind what part of them you will use, and begin to write the book which will make your vast knowledge useful to the world?" (Ch. 20). Casaubon is unable to profit from his bitter discovery that his wife has a mind of her own, and withdraws into the familiar regions of social convention designed to preserve the supremacy of the male ego. He uses the decrees of society, both legal and unspoken, to circumscribe Dorothea's life after his death, adding to his will the codicil by which Dorothea would lose her estate if she remarries. The weight of social opinion seemed to be strongly in favor of a woman remaining devoted, so to speak, to the memory of her dead husband. In *Middlemarch* the issue of disinheritance figures strikingly in relation to two other women besides Dorothea. Ladislaw's grandmother, whose miniature had always fascinated Dorothea, was disinherited "because she made what they called a mésalliance" (Ch. 37); while Mary Garth refuses to accede to Featherstone's wishes at his deathbed (Ch. 33) and loses a fortune too. Casaubon does not rely on this legal sanction alone; he would wring an actual promise out of Dorothea not to marry again (Ch. 48). In the event, she is spared a response, but the point is made: should a woman's subjection in marriage go so far? In a marriage which has hung "like a murder" (Ch. 81), the momentary flicker of rapport between husband and wife at the end of Chapter 42 is one of the most moving passages in the entire novel, and affords a remarkably convincing illustration of the fruits of Dorothea's womanly power.

Lydgate's story is more chilling owing to the ease with which Rosamond overcomes a man of his intellectual caliber. She begins her act of destruction with "Do you know, Tertius, I often wish you had not been a medical man" (Ch. 45); and no worthwhile affection lightens the history of this marriage. Unlike Casaubon, Lydgate is resilient enough to seek a way out of his impasse, but his appeal to Rosamond is doomed, for she replies in her most "neutral" way, "What can *I* do, Tertius?" (author's italics). Dorothea had addressed an almost identically worded question to Casaubon, "What shall I do?" and the range between the two questions is the subject of authorial comment:

> That little speech [of Rosamond's] of four words, like so many others in all languages, is capable by varied vocal inflexions of expressing all states of mind from helpless dimness to exhaustive argumentative perception, from the completest self-devoting fellowship to the most neutral aloofness. (Ch. 58)

In other words, in both marriages the force of intellect, the traditional preserve of the man, is baffled by grinding female skepticism, aroused partly by undervalued potential.

The critical gap in the relations between Dorothea and Lydgate, then, does not present a simple unrelated contrast but is the locus of a creatively balanced interplay of character and of an organic extension of theme. To extend this line of argument to include Ladislaw, however, is admittedly much more debatable. What is clear is that against the reality of the two failed marriages which also represent a great novelist's response to issues of the day, the relationship of Dorothea and Ladislaw has a tinsel charm so incredibly at variance that it is unreasonable to interpret it as a failure of authorial distancing—and at the finishing line at that. Does it strain credulity to accept this conclusion rather as a sop to contemporary readers who had watched the dramas of married life unfold month by month over 1871–82? The implausible innocence of this pair may have been intended partly as a "consoling lie" (to borrow a phrase from Barbara Hardy), and the source of the artistic failure may well lie in an attenuation of concern for the novel's internal laws by the demands of popular publishing. Still the romantic conclusion is double-edged, and accords with the present argument: by finally allying Ladislaw's limited romanticism with Dorothea's "vigorous enthusiasm" (Ch. 19), shallow notions of romantic love are also ironically placed. The romantic ending to Dorothea's career stands in contrast to her true potential, as well as to the thoroughgoing analysis of love and marriage which informs most of the book. This concluding symmetrical touch, so far as it concerns Ladislaw, remains obstinately skeletal in the total pattern of character relationships, it is true, but at the least we can see it as a failure of art, rather than of sensibility.

Of course the characterization of Dorothea was something close to the author's heart, but so too, one needs must see, was the issue so judiciously espoused and so diversely hidden. Its undeniable presence nevertheless makes it clear that the character of Lydgate contributes importantly to the structure of the novel. He is the linchpin for the intricate scientific and social world of Middlemarch as Dorothea is for its best, though inarticulate, aspirations. That these two are themselves bound to each other by a profound though unnamed kinship, recalling George Eliot's ideal of the integration of feeling and intellect, is as much an enlightening commentary on a vexed social issue as a highly successful artistic device which unobtrusively secures the novel as a whole. W. J. Harvey was right to say that with George Eliot "We do not leave the 'real' world behind when we are confronted with the world of the novels; in fact [she] compels us to keep both worlds firmly in our minds."[30]

Middlemarch is the complete embodiment of sound, conservative, mid-Victorian reaction to the movement for women's freedom. It bears witness to the author's desire to accommodate, within the traditional ethic, the changes it heralded. Aligning herself with the most constructive thinking of the times, she created a heroine whose great intellectual and passional vitality cannot be fully understood except as a major contribution to the revaluation, which had now begun, of the nature and role of women in society. Approached in this way, the novel reveals an even more highly organized pattern of structural relationships among the five major characters than has been recognized. It exposes the hollowness of contemporary notions of womanliness while at the same time satirizing male-oriented conventions in marriage and law. George Meredith was to take up the theme of male egoism only five years later. His searching analysis of its power to destroy human dignity entirely justified the criticisms George Eliot had leveled at it.

George Eliot treated lifelong marriage as the crucial fact of life, but potentially tragic in essence. Marriage could alleviate the fundamental sense of isolation which human beings feel in a universe unfriendly to individual hopes; but it rarely succeeded, partly for reasons beyond human control, but also because the potential contribution of women toward successful unions had been underestimated. Despite the dramatic impact of the theme of marital incompatibility, George Eliot would not concede one major point of morality regarding marriage. As she said, women's freedom threatened "abysses"— meaning, no doubt, the more or less complete overthrow of the existing sexual ethic. Divorce is therefore not a way out for her, and much of her pessimism arises from her realization of the cost, in human terms, of accepting the irrevocable nature of the marriage bond. Yet in *Daniel Deronda* she was to give the impossibility of release from the bond a near-tragic dimension through Gwendolen's tormenting desire to see her husband destroyed. This last novel was also to reiterate the importance of self-scrutiny for women, even as it conducted its most searching examination of decayed social mores against a vision of the human sensibility as it might develop in future generations.

III

As a final, mature statement of George Eliot's interests and concerns in the latter part of her career, *Daniel Deronda* (1876) does not disappoint, even despite our longstanding difficulties with what she called "the Jewish element" (*Letters,* VI, 238). Her scrutiny of intersexual relations is even more piercing than in *Middlemarch,* her fictional technique in the justly praised first two-thirds of the novel has been honed to yield a fresh pitch of dramatic intensity, while her vision has expanded to embrace the entire human race including other oppressed groups besides women—Jews, blacks, and "half-breeds" (Ch. 29). She chose for her scope a range which extends from the rooted particular to visionary dreams and images. In terms of technique she sought to go beyond the conventional bounds of realism to include an emotionally persuasive style which would give life to the nebulous ideals of the race as a whole. In her ambitious program she achieved a degree of success allowed only to the greatest writers. An important part of her purpose was the establishment of a wide perspective within which continuity and change with respect to the place of women might be more truly assessed. "Girls and their blind visions" were to be located in a context where "ideas were with fresh vigour making armies of themselves, and the universal kinship was declaring itself fiercely" (Ch. 11). The point is reiterated in the penultimate chapter of the novel when Gwendolen realizes that her own drama had been "reduced to a mere speck" before the "bewildering vision of . . . wide-stretching purposes" (Ch. 69).

Perhaps the very vastness of this scope has discouraged close examination of how the position of women gives the novel some of its key emphases. For George Eliot, women's problems were always part of larger ethical issues confronting the society as a whole. In *Daniel Deronda* these problems are given a more acute definition in the characterization of Gwendolen, and in the subtle contrast of the prison which is her marriage as against the extramarital union of Grandcourt and Lydia Glasher. At the same time, the author's treatment of Deronda and Mordecai represents a bold challenge to her readers to recognize the importance of using "emotional intellect" (Ch. 41) to resolve the apparently insoluble moral dilemmas which have been dramatized. An explication of these concerns should bring into a more balanced perspective the novel's achievements and its excesses, and so help bind its two main disparate parts rather more plausibly, if still not completely. One noted in *Middlemarch* how the realistic and persuasive elements had been brought, in the person of Dorothea, to an optimum point in relation to each other. But George Eliot was not content with merely aesthetic wholeness, however satisfying. In her last novel her creative energies sought a fresh, more ambitious variant in the relation between the realistic and the persuasive, one that would suffuse not just a single character but the entire work. In an essay entitled "Historic Imagination," she said she wanted "something different from the schemed picturesqueness of ordinary historical fiction," that she required "freedom from the vulgar coercion of conventional plot."[31] By the exercise of a "veracious" imagination, an author could "help the judgement greatly with regard to present and future events."

In the sense that George Eliot was not content only to interpret her world, but also sought to change it, her novels are indeed "social acts."[32] While they do not propose political action to bring about preferred changes in society, they are designed to influence the sensibility toward action beneficial to the community. Seen schematically, Daniel Deronda finds his vocation as the agent of change on this large scale, Gwendolen Harleth learns through him the need to ally her petty purposes to the benignant tendencies of life, while Henleigh Grandcourt is the personification of a society in decay, yet completely resistant to change. Grandcourt and Deronda represent the real and ideal worlds which do not touch, while the woman is the medium through whom the painful process of indictment and regeneration, individual as well as social, is enacted. Her personal odyssey, narrated with unsurpassed dramatic skill, is emblematic of the race growing to an awareness of the need to move from the deadness of the present to the utopian vision. In conception if rather less in execution, she is at the center of the process of ameliorative change.

Gwendolen is directly in the line from Rosamond Vincy of *Middlemarch* and Lucy Deane of *The Mill on the Floss,* while standing as a worthy counterpart to Dorothea Brooke. Ironic distancing in the portrayal of Rosamond had led the *Spectator* to believe that there was malice on the part of the author toward the type of " 'nice, superficial conventional young ladies" whom Rosamond represented.[33] Actually, apart from the purposes of *Middlemarch,* Rosamond's is only a partial portrait which does not venture beyond the suggestion that her deep-seated malice arises from boredom with everything. In choosing to anatomize the malaise through Gwendolen and in tracing her rescue back to the path of responsible living, George Eliot demonstrates the greater completeness of her response to the problems of the middle-class women of her time. As a perceptive contemporary critic suggested, Gwendolen is Rosamond Vincy endowed "with a soul."[34] There is another way in which this last heroine completes George Eliot's gallery of women. Although Dorothea Brooke is often regarded as the most brilliant of them all, her luminous presence had nevertheless an air of being partly drawn to a manifesto. Gwendolen is a figure of comparable stature but completely identifiable with the society of her author's time. In scrutinizing the one, we discover that inimical features of the other are exposed as well. The subjection of women in marriage together with the conditions which nurture that subjection undergo searching examination in a work of immense power.

Unlike Dorothea but like Rosamond, Gwendolen has no lineage in any historic current of energy. Her solitary playful wish to "be Saint Cecilia," the patron saint of music (Ch. 3), is repudiated with brutal precision by Klesmer, who indicts what she sings (Ch. 5) and how she approaches the art (Ch. 23). "That music which you sing is beneath you," he tells her. "It is a form of melody which expresses a puerile state of culture—a dangling, canting, see-saw kind of stuff" (Ch. 3). The occasion being a social one, Klesmer is careful to confine most of his remarks to the music rather than the performer, although his double-edged "It is always acceptable to hear you sing" is not lost on her. His strictures on the music as reflecting "a sort of self-satisfied folly . . . [with] no sense of the universal" apply with equal force to the society which fosters complacent values and to the singer who is content with no more. With the decline of the family fortunes, when Gwendolen thinks seriously of taking up singing as a career, she invites Klesmer's most biting evaluation of her own personality and upbringing. Itemizing the "three terrible musts" which she has ignored (exactness in knowing, understanding, and doing), he tells her bluntly, "You have not been called upon to be anything but a charming young lady" (Ch. 23). He teaches her the distinction between mere accomplishment and genuine artistry. She lacks "inward vocation," she has never subdued her mind and body to "unbroken discipline," she has never had any real training or instruction. She is a "mediocrity."

A similar but rather more complex exposé of Gwendolen's acting pretensions takes place at the same time. Gwendolen seems to make a glib assumption that, being a lady trained in the conventional social arts, she can make the transition from real life to the stage with relative ease. She has been brought up to act a part in real life and believes the stage will not call upon her to do very much more than that. She is the victim of her own unconscious irony as Klesmer pointedly undeceives her. A woman who would rely on "the unquestioned power of her beauty as a passport [to the stage]," he tells her, ". . . is usually one who thinks of entering on a luxurious life by a short and easy road—perhaps by marriage" (Ch. 23). For the stage too one must be taught—"trained to bear [oneself] on the stage, as a horse, however beautiful, must be trained for the circus." Gwendolen is denied the rigors of the legitimate theater but she does not escape acting out her own marriage drama in real life. After her marriage to Grandcourt she is forcibly "brought to kneel down like a horse under training for the arena" (Ch. 28).[35] Gwendolen's encounters with Klesmer are wonderfully controlled pieces of dramatic writing, subtly taking apart the artifice in her personality and revealing a disconcerting hollowness at the core.

The strongest indication of George Eliot's sympathy for the character, however, is the entirely convincing representation of Gwendolen's growing conscience and the strong affirmation, which constitutes the novel's substance, of her capability for redemption. She is not "well rooted in some spot of native land" (Ch. 3), her talents are exercised "from the drawing-room *standpunkt*" (Ch. 23), she dislikes anything religious, and she has a "blank indifference" (Ch. 6) toward everyone and everything. "Be as cross with me as you like—only don't treat me with indifference," Rex Gascoigne implores her, but she repudiates him. Overcome by the sense of her aversion to love, side by side with her enjoyment of the homage men pay to her beauty, she breaks down, sobbing, "I shall never love anybody. I can't love people. I hate them" (Ch. 7). Mrs. Gascoigne and, later, Daniel Deronda, not fully understanding her, suspect she has "the heart of a coquette" (Chs. 8, 35). But her coquetry is different from that of Sue Bridehead in Hardy's *Jude the Obscure.* Like Hermione of *The Winter's Tale,* whose part she plays in the amateur theatricals at Offendene (Ch. 6), Gwendolen appears to be as dead as a statue and is restored to wholeness only at the end of her harrowing marriage.

No one at first understands the meaning of Gwendolen's periodic bouts of hysterical screaming. They are indications of a kind of existential anxiety, an involuntary panic brought about by an awareness of spiritual barrenness, and of the need to "care for something in this vast world besides the gratification of small selfish desires" (Ch. 36). Gwendolen anticipates George Moore's Mildred Lawson, a much lesser figure, and of course Ibsen's Hedda Gabler, but what distinguishes her from her successors is her inarticulate craving for contact with the infinite universe. Mildred Lawson and Hedda Gabler are much more purely aesthetic creations, drawn in an age which had lost not only religious belief but even George Eliot's great capacity for an all-embracing "constituting sympathy" in a confusing world.

But one must guard against the temptation to read this novel mainly as an account of the regenerative process in Gwendolen. Her crucible is her marriage. The marriage itself is not just another illustration of the theme of marital incompatibility (although it is that also, to an excruciating degree), it is the symbol of the dead heart of a culture which had failed to look inward. Grandcourt, Gwendolen's husband, has been described as "the one irretrievably lost soul in George Eliot's fiction."[36] The reptilian imagery used to picture the destructive nonchalance of his entire personality (lizard, alligator, boa constrictor, serpent) reinforces the sense of a baleful presence which cannot be wished away.[37] Grandcourt's menacing languor is more than a match for Gwendolen's "blank indifference." He represents a landowning aristocracy which believes in the permanence of its social structure and the irrevocability of its conventions. Politics holds no interest for him because, as "a man of position and weight" (Ch. 44), his standing in the community is assured. "He is not ridiculous," says Gwendolen, speaking truer than she knows (Ch. 11). Without even a slight "ridiculousness," Grandcourt is case-hardened; his style is the man. He always "knew what to say" (Ch. 29), giving Gwendolen "neatly turned compliments" (Ch. 35) before their marriage, and after it lending words "the power of thumbscrews and the cold touch of the rack" (Ch. 54). There is a cruel aptness in their coming together. He is the prize for which her entire upbringing has prepared her, the promise of "the rank and luxuries" (Ch. 54) she could naturally expect. For her part she is the sleek, restive beauty, who by her accomplishments is an acquisiton in the eyes of society, and whom it fascinates him to subdue, the more because she "would have liked to master him" (Ch. 28). Gwendolen, who had spent a lot of time in front of her mirror, even kissing her own image (Ch. 2), eventually finds herself in a wilderness of mirrors in her yacht cabin on the Mediterranean, mocked by the unreal images by which she has lived.[38] The narcissistic partners are in a prison from which there is no escape.

Seen in this light, Gwendolen's murderous intent toward Grandcourt assumes a symbolic function hinting at a revolutionary readiness to destroy something which survives only as "a contract" (Ch. 54), no more. In *Middlemarch* the marriages of Dorothea and Lydgate had at least been lightened by positive strivings toward self-adjustment, however difficult. The complete lack of substance in the marriage of Gwendolen and Grandcourt is George Eliot's most emphatic undermining of the convention of lifelong permanence in the bond which was a cornerstone of her society. But if her attack had been confined to the fact of the imprisonment to which the partners were condemned, and to the hollowness of a bond entered into on the ground that appearances alone were all-important, it might have been possible to argue that her indictment was incomplete, or pleaded special exceptions. Gwendolen might, in a moment of strength, resolve "to wear the yoke so as not to be pitied" (Ch. 35), but she is afflicted by insidious doubt that Grandcourt's liaison with Mrs. Glasher has a prior claim to recognition as his true marital commitment. No doubt her conscience is partly wracked by her broken promise to Lydia Glasher at their meeting at the Whispering Stones that she would not marry Grandcourt (Ch. 14). But she cannot expunge from her mind Lydia's words in the letter which accompanied Grandcourt's gift of the diamonds:

> "The man you have married has a withered heart. His best young love was mine; you could not take that from me when you took the rest. It is dead; but I am the grave in which your chance of happiness is buried. . . . The willing wrong you have done me will be your curse." (Ch. 35)

The dramatic juxtaposition of Grandcourt's two unions, one extramarital but sanctioned by a ten-year association and four children, the other formally recognized as having exclusive legal validity, is George Eliot's final assault on the bastion of Victorian marriage and its conventions. The irony of the contrast is secondary to the insistent suggestion that the union with Lydia Glasher is the truer marriage. Lydia's standpoint is not simply that of the jilted lover deserving compassion. Grandcourt had once been willing to marry her but her husband had not consented to a divorce, "not wishing to have his domestic habits printed in evidence" (Ch. 30). Lydia believes that if Gwendolen had not appeared on the scene Grandcourt would eventually have come round to marrying her, legitimizing her standing and their children's, and making their son Henleigh his heir. The contrast of the extramarital union with the legal marriage is highlighted by Grandcourt's diamonds, which become a symbol raising doubts about which of the two women, Lydia or Gwendolen, should be regarded as their rightful custodian and hence Grandcourt's true marriage partner. In an involuntary gesture repudiating her own claim and thereby the validity of her own marriage, Gwendolen casts the jewels to the floor, screaming hysterically when she sees Grandcourt walk into her room on the night of their wedding (Ch. 31).

Yet it was not absoluteness of a contrary kind which George Eliot sought to advance. To her clear-eyed vision even unions based on passionate love grew stale. "You are very attractive, Miss Harleth," Lydia says. "But when he first knew me I too was young" (Ch. 14). If neither passion nor law could promise lasting happiness in marriage, those entering into it are embarking on a gamble. Gwendolen, who has gambled at Leubronn, gambles with similar recklessness in marrying Grandcourt, "daring everything to win much—or if to lose, still with *èclat* and a sense of importance" (Ch. 31). She who, like Grandcourt, would make style the criterion of everything, is reminded by Deronda of the moral core in her nature which she has ignored. She not only hurts Lydia by ignoring her claims; she has also done a hurt to an inviolable part of herself. As she admits much later, "I wanted to make my gain out of another's loss—it was like roulette . . . and I had won . . . I knew I was guilty" (Ch. 56).

The other set of jewels in the novel, the turquoise necklace pawned by Gwendolen, redeemed and returned to her by Deronda, stands for a hidden capacity, present in everyone, for relying on qualities of greater permanence to cope with individual human faithlessness (one's own or another's) as much as with the obstinacy of withered social norms. George Eliot contrasts the symbolism of the necklace with that of the Grandcourt diamonds with consummate dramatic skill. Without knowing exactly why, Gwendolen will not let the necklace go again after its rescue from the jewelry dealer. It becomes the object of a fierce battle between her and Grandcourt whether she should wear his gift or her own heirloom (Ch. 36). Defeated, she submits to his fastening the diamonds (like a halter) around her neck, but she defiantly winds her own necklace around her wrist hidden under the glove, for the sake of Deronda. By that gesture she indicates her instinctive refusal to surrender her capacity for moral growth and moral choice, even in a world in which subjugation is total and from which there appears to be no escape. Under Deronda's tutelage she will come to realize that "the word of all work Love" (Ch. 27) extends its range far beyond the mere "centaur power" (Ch. 7), by which she has lived, to outer reaches of meaning which offer the only hope for transcending the hard realities of her lot. She will learn that her oppressive sense of "inward darkness" (her guilt as well as her subjection) may be assuaged by nurturing "the star-like out-glowing of some pure fellow-feeling" based on a supreme kind of selflessness (Ch. 69).

Here we reach the world of Deronda and George Eliot's final

attempt to give to her theory of integrated sensibility—"emotional intellect" (Ch. 41)—a place, in fiction as much as in life, consonant with the moral force which she believed it had. The thoroughgoing effort to represent this faculty artistically as well as persuasively gives to *Daniel Deronda* the air of being an experimental Victorian novel. The experiment fails because the idea of a tradition for the emotional yearnings of the human race is only barely distinguishable from the specific Judaic tradition. One cannot imagine an author like George Eliot being unaware of the artistic risks of placing such a heavy emphasis on any specific spiritual tradition, and it will be worthwhile trying to discern just what she sought to do. There will be no need to repeat the many strictures leveled at "the Jewish element" of *Daniel Deronda* since its first publication. Of the fewer sympathetic views, the *Gentleman's Magazine* described the novel as "a grand romance of the woman's soul, in the highest sense of the word."[39] The writer, R. E. Francillon, defined "romance" as a work which "grapples with fact upon its whole ground, and deals with the higher and wider truths—the more occult wisdom—that is not to be picked up by the side of the highway." This is a good way to introduce a hypothesis about the book's structure as a deliberate three-stage fading away from concrete reality and toward an abstract religious condition. In the first concrete stage is Gwendolen's solidly realized world; in the intermediate stage is Deronda's pursuit of his true heritage and of an ideology for living which would be in harmony with the ideal of "the ultimate unity of mankind" (Ch. 61); and in the final stage is Mordecai's "philosophical-allegorical-mystical" belief (Ch. 52) in a condition of selflessness in which all religions and nations participate.

The first stage takes us up to the end of Chapter 36 (about a third of the way through Book V). The second and third stages are not consecutive but rather, to use cinema terminology, cross-faded, reaching a climax in Mordecai's abstruseness in Chapter 40. Of the last thirty chapters of the novel, only eight can really be said to deal with Gwendolen (Chs. 48, 54–59, 69); the rest are devoted to the attempt to breathe dramatic life into Deronda's own search for his identity and his relations with his new community, with Mordecai's visions in the background, depicted with the "Turneresque splendour of sunset."[40] There is a slight dramatic interlinking of the first and second stages, that is, of Gwendolen's moral progress and Deronda's quest. They meet, as Dorothea and Lydgate do, after they are committed to distinctly separate paths (Ch. 29), and she is aware that her marriage to Grandcourt had dimmed his chances of being made Sir Hugo's heir to Topping Abbey. Any further potential in this dramatic irony of their meeting is dissipated by the author's resolute characterization of Deronda as a disinterested adviser. Sir Hugo wonders whether Deronda is playing with fire in his frequent meetings with Gwendolen, but Deronda's reply is dismally true: there is nothing answering Sir Hugo's metaphor, he says—"no fire, and therefore no chance of scorching" (Ch. 36).

In making Deronda represent pure feeling, George Eliot does establish the point that it is not the prerogative of the female sex alone, but in seeking to give it undiluted human presence through Deronda and Mordecai she seems to have completely overestimated the degree to which the novel can bear a persuasive function. Her proportionate emphasis on her three-stage structure appears to be based on a misconception that the importance of feeling could be aptly demonstrated only by making the space devoted to it nearly co-extensive with the realistic narrative. As one writer drily remarked, if George Eliot had been content to "give us her word for Deronda, to elaborate him less, she would have accomplished more."[41] The effect of the co-extensive treatment serves only to achieve the opposite of what was intended—instead of making Deronda's interests impinge more credibly on Gwendolen's, it accentuates the distance between them, perhaps to the breaking point.

On feeling inself, the novel offers an anatomy of this all-embracing word with a systematically increasing intensity which has not been sufficiently noticed, let alone appreciated. The stages of feeling dramatized by Deronda and Mordecai are remarkably parallel to the system of thought reconstructed from the *Letters* in the first section of this chapter, but going beyond that system into mystical realms. To begin with, feeling is "as inherited yearning—the effect of brooding, passionate thoughts in many ancestors" (Ch. 63). It is to be distinguished from strict reasoning, which itself is not exempt from "false conclusions and illusory speculations" (Ch. 41). Knowledge needs to be gathered up into one current with the emotions (Ch. 32), and the sensibility used "as if it were a faculty, like vision" (Ch. 36). The individual is obliged to nurture this faculty within himself, seeking at the same time to apply its promptings on the social scale. This dual process is a form of "poetic energy" (Dorothea's kind, not Ladislaw's) which may be used to cope with the recurring challenge to people in every age to identify and discard "enshrined putrefactions" in their society, and align themselves with "the faint beginnings" of new, ameliorating trends (Ch. 32). What interests us here is the author's effort to provide a fundamental rationale for the rebel in society. Deronda emphasizes that this kind of social awareness is different from political action (Ch. 33), because it is based on "affection [which] is the broadest basis of good in life" (Ch. 35). Through discipline and "fixed meditation" one may progress in defining "our longing or dread" (Ch. 36), and thus assist in "the transmutation of self" to a condition of selflessness akin to that advocated by "Bouddha" (Ch. 37).

Mordecai is the spokesman for what happens at this ideal level. An individual who has achieved the selfless state acquires "a foreshadowing power" by which, presumably, he is able to distinguish fresh growth from old decay in human life. Mordecai's own "coherent trains of thought often resembled the significant dreams attributed to sleepers by waking persons in their most inventive moments" (Ch. 38). In this advanced stage, the sensibility operates through images and dreams, yielding "visions (which) are the creators and feeders of the world" and bordering on "the breadth of divine thought" (Ch. 40). The personality achieves a release, "as it were to mingle with the ocean of human existence, free from the pressure of individual bondage" (Ch. 43). There, soul melts into soul and the best thoughts and ideas are conveyed from generation to generation (Ch. 63). There is a whiff of a kind of Victorian *Finnegans Wake* when Mordecai is about.

While this reads like a universal progress of the soul, George Eliot sought to illustrate its chief elements in parallel fashion on the social scale. The attempt was to be the source of her undoing. Deronda longs to be "an organic part of social life, instead of roaming in it like a yearning disembodied spirit" (Ch. 32). Gwendolen's marriage interests him because he wishes to affect the lives of people like her "with some sort of redeeming influence" (Ch. 28). She receives much useful practical advice from him on widening her interests by allowing her sensibility greater scope for action—which seems to be the principal (if not the sole) exemplification of the operations of the "emotional intellect" (Ch. 41) in the real, concrete world. His advice recalls much that George Eliot recommended to the women of her time, in her letters, about steps they should themselves take for improving their lot. "Look on other lives besides your own," Deronda counsels; cultivate an interest "beyond the small drama of personal desires," discover an occupation which "you [can] care about with passionate delight or even independent interest" (Ch.

36). But when it comes to action on the social scale George Eliot surrenders completely her wise distinction between social and political action, making the prophecy that with the establishment of Israel "there will be a land set for a halting-place of enmities" (Ch. 42). It is not the particular nation chosen—indeed no particular nation can be chosen without contradicting unwritten but fundamental literary laws—nor the absurdity of the prophecy, nor yet again the present patent falsity of the prophecy which causes the difficulty. It is that all the author's safeguards against excessive special pleading for oppressed groups, whether women or Jews, are suddenly and totally relinquished, and despite her own convictions, political action becomes the way to revive the "organic centre" of mankind (Ch. 42) on the social as well as spiritual levels. Mordecai, who is her spokesman, sacrifices visionary conviction for a quite ordinary partisanship.

As a philosophical novel *Daniel Deronda* illustrates what George Saintsbury called "the immutable law that no perfect novel can ever be written in designed illustration of a theory, whether moral or immoral."[42] The perfect novel was not George Eliot's quarry. Her penetrating study of the condition of women exposes "enshrined putrefactions" but deliberately sacrifices aesthetic shape and balance in order to place women in a context of the highest spiritual ideals. In the process, the moral conventions of the day are not the only casualty. The conventions of the Victorian novel itself fall away. Perhaps it is this dual rebellion which makes us come back again and again to this novel. It affords a great instance of an author in rebellion against the conventions of society rebelling ultimately against the orthodox conventions of her art as well. And, to use George Eliot's own criterion for judging an author who aimed at more than temporary influence, the novel has after all "that salt of a noble *enthusiasm* which . . . rebukes our critical discrimination."[43]

IV

The contemporary social meanings of George Eliot's works are not separable from her literary art. Indeed, the proper appreciation of such meanings actually deepens our understanding of her technique, style, and overall achievement. *The Mill on the Floss, Middlemarch,* and *Daniel Deronda* deal centrally with the moral issues of women's freedom in a static society. They rest on aspects of a profound theory of the human sensibility which gives an equal place to the contribution women can make to the quality of life. In general terms, *The Mill on the Floss* studies the conflict between a woman's actions, undertaken with integrity, and the traditional norms of her upbringing. It ends with the suggestion that while the past is to be respected, the prospect of changes in received wisdom cannot be avoided. On the other hand, the pioneer, carried on the tide of feeling, must be alert to the hazard of totally independent action—she will cut herself off from the mainstream of human growth and development. The structure of *Middlemarch* rests on the author's twin concepts of feeling and intellect, giving dramatic life to both, and revealing how the contribution of women can be grossly underestimated, as in Dorothea, or disfigured and suppressed, as in Rosamond. The study of their marriages highlights the crux of the Victorian problem of the relations between the sexes. Where partners are incompatible but bound to each other for life, only great resources of feeling and human fellowship can bear them along—but even then only very inadequately.

While *The Mill on the Floss* is concerned with redefining a relationship to the past, *Middlemarch* is much more contemporary in its tone and impact. *Daniel Deronda* continues the momentum into the future, examining present tragedy against a vision of regenerated human affection. It indicts Victorian culture itself through its central institution of marriage, with an unexcelled degree of social and moral penetration. The novel resolutely proposes no practical alternatives but looks toward an ideal future when the oppressiveness of current mores will have been left behind. Equally it emphasizes the searching self-scrutiny in which women must engage if they are to make a significant contribution to the race as a whole. *Daniel Deronda* marks not only the end of the author's novelistic career but also the end of an era. Its magnificent vision is testament to the generous hope of an older generation, though not an admission of the striking changes in sexual mores which were to come. The novel in George Eliot's hands depicts the relations between the sexes, especially in marriage, primarily in social and spiritual terms. She takes the physical aspects for granted (apart from discreet references to Casaubon's impotence), seeming to assume that vagaries under this head are of less importance when compared to the "right" mental approach to the union. In the novelists who followed, we find this attitude gradually weakening, until at the climax of the period under study, Hardy's *Jude the Obscure* feverishly reverses George Eliot's emphasis to acknowledge the equally fundamental moral difficulties presented by the vagaries of the flesh.

3 Meredith: Liberation, Morality, and Style

There are two chief reasons why George Meredith has claims to our attention. He was a brilliant and sophisticated experimenter in the art of the novel; and his scrutiny of English society, especially its upper echelons, has rarely been equaled in depth. Both these factors are inseparable from his treatment of questions regarding the moral status and the rights and responsibilities of women. In a secular framework he gave women an importance similar to that which George Eliot had given them in a philosophical one. His thought deserves consideration for its humane regard for all classes of persons; his work, for the social imagination which breathes individual life into his characters while binding them together. Still his novels are marred, as F. N. Lees has pointed out in an admirable essay, "by a wavering grasp of technique and by difficulty of style" which deter most nonacademic readers nowadays.[1] The literary method worked up to a degree of opaqueness, in Meredith's later novels, that is an admitted trial to patience. We have been inured to more challenging experiments in the twentieth century, it is true, but this is at best a negative defense. Meredith is the first English novelist to try to lend substance to the very concept of a secular morality, and it is not surprising that his pioneering efforts should have achieved only qualified success.

From a literary point of view, in Meredith's novels the technique is the thing. In essentials, the literary method in *The Egoist* (1879), *Diana of the Crossways* (1885), and *One of Our Conquerors* (1891) represents a progressively tortuous search for a form of words which would describe in more readily acceptable terms changes heralded by emancipationist agitation. The tortuousness itself, from which even *The Egoist* is not wholly exempt, is as much a mark of strong sympathy for the movement as it is of an excessive concession to conservative views. These novels, which typify between them the interests and the achievement of Meredith's later career, will be examined for the extent to which his method was affected by four themes in particular: his adaptation of Realistic tenets for presenting truths of sexual emotion raised by feminist agitation; his sympathy for women who attempted to make independent decisions regarding their marriage partners; his critique of male attitudes which contribute to the subjugation of women; and his efforts to represent the actual substance of the social fabric of which the three foregoing themes are a part.

I

Current controversies over Realism throw some light on the unresolved creative problem implicit in Meredith's novels. While the example of the French Realists was found on the whole to be unacceptable on the English scene, writers began to deal more frankly than in the past with matters concerning relations between the sexes. All of Meredith's novels show that he took the challenge of Realism very much in his stride: he rejected its major pretensions. He refused to adopt "the custom of our period (called the Realistic) to create, when casual opportunity offers, a belief in the narrative by promoting nausea in the audience" (*One of Our Conquerors*, Ch. 19). He was no prude—though it would have been very easy for a person of his generation to be one. His own good taste and decency reflect worthy Victorian ideals before they become distorted. In upholding them he did not shirk the plain facts of sex and sexual relationships, an attitude which makes his unceasing search for a delicate proportion between good taste and the "whole" truth admirable even today. "No realism frightens me," he told W. E. Henley. "At its worst, I take it as a correction of the flimsy to which our literature has a constant tendency to recur. Even the lowest appears to me more instructive than Byronics."[2] This issues directly from his general philosophical and moral position:

> I have written always with the perception that there is no life but of the spirit; that the concrete is really the shadowy; yet that the way to spiritual life lies in the complete unfolding of the creature, not in the nipping of his passions.[3]

Meredith's commonsense attitude to truths about the nature of human beings and their desires has an essential basis of psychological truth. In Chapter 1 of *Diana of the Crossways* he comments that basic human nature may be ugly, but we ignore it at our peril, since if we support ideals alone, "an unfailing aboriginal democratic old monster . . . waits to pull us down." Should we be compelled to make a choice, it would be wiser to "shun the grossness of the over-dainty" and choose Realistic truth, "for nature will force her way, and if you try to stifle her by drowning, she comes up, not the fairest part of her uppermost!" This acknowledgment of aspects of life, hitherto taboo, as part of a more reasonable foundation for human ideals marks an intermediate stage in the changes in literary and social attitudes then taking place. Meredith incorporated, especially in his later novels, truths of sexual emotion, but he never believed that detail in the manner of the Realists served any useful purpose. His objections to them were twofold. Their vogue depended excessively on unpleasant physical detail; if this implied a theory of truth, the theory was a false one. They also offended good taste. His style accords closely with this position.

To cover the physical facts of human life generally unpalatable to Victorian readers, Meredith relied extensively on images from nature. He took special care to use nature images in profusion when presenting an idea which would ordinarily jar conventional tastes, as in Chapter 16 of *Diana of the Crossways* in which Dacier discovers the heroine early one morning standing by a pool in the lakelands of North Italy and discreetly withdraws, convinced that "she who found her pleasure in these haunts of nymph and goddess, at the fresh cold bosom of nature, must be clear as day"; thenceforth, despite the suit for divorce pending against her, he is "ready to side with the evidence declaring her free from stain." The chapter clarifies some of Meredith's creative intentions. He wanted to correct the moral myopia of his readers, and shift them from petrified principles of social evaluation, which automatically condemned a woman like Diana, to "natural" criteria of judgment. He meant to dissolve the attachment to longstanding anchors of conduct—"the scales of convention, the mud-spots of accident" (*One of Our Conquerors,* Ch. 28)—and replace them with a sense felt intuitively to be in harmony with Nature. He did not seek to argue but to persuade with accumulated suggestions of beauty. In *The Egoist,* Vernon Whitford half-dozing under the cherry tree and Clara peeping down at him are momentarily united in a common vision of beautiful nature which makes them acknowledge, at the same time it partly justifies, their physical emotions. They are, in fact, symbolically on the verge of a sexual embrace, and are able, fleetingly, to accept this without the taboos with which it was normally hedged. Caution prevented Meredith from going further; in the 1870s it was sufficient to suggest a vision heralding the disappearance of old taboos, something to "play at rich and poor with," not to be prematurely codified:

> It is the golden key of all the possible: new worlds expand beneath the dawn it brings us. Just outside reality, it illumines, enriches, and softens real things;—and to desire it in preference to the simple fact, is a damning proof of enervation. (Ch. 12)

This approach to sexual themes in the novel was for a time a positive alternative to the method of the Realists. Images of open air, rain, lakes, rivers, mountains, cherry tree, and so on, reminded readers unobtrusively of aspects in life they were prone to fear or discount. Sexual feelings are "natural"—part of nature. The bracing pleasantness of natural surroundings exorcised repugnance and suggested that the tactful acknowledgment of sexuality was preferable to feelings of shame and secrecy. We have W. E. Henley's testimony that Meredith succeeded in his intentions unambiguously in *The Egoist:* "Meredith has considered sex—the great subject, the leaven of imaginative art—with notable audacity and insight."[4] Less inhibited sensibilities today are more likely to regard Meredith's approach as a shade too idealistic, his vision too prettified. His images provoke but do not satisfy a curiosity about the real facts intended by the usage in each instance. Especially in *The Egoist* and *Diana of the Crossways,* which are suggestive in part, the metaphors lose some of their effect through persisting isolation from the human facts they are meant to identify. Too often, they seem, in accumulation, like a screen made deliberately impenetrable.

Meredith did bring a greater degree of sophistication to his use of nature in *One of Our Conquerors,* suggesting that it could not be easily separated from mere promiscuity. While Radnor's action in deserting his wife for one he really loves accords with nature, as does Nataly's in consenting to live with him, how were these to be distinguished from responses to mere wayward instinct? During a holiday cruise, Radnor engages in dalliance with the experienced Lady Grace Halley upon receiving "an impulsive squeeze of fingers." Meredith writes, ironically,

> The gentleman was taught to feel that an ever so slightly lengthened compression of the hand female shoots within us

both straight and far and round the corners. There you have Nature, if you want her naked in her elements, for a text. He loved his Nataly truly, even fervently, after the twenty years of union; he looked about at no other woman; it happened only that the touch of one, the chance warm touch, put to motion the blind forces of our mother so remarkably surcharging him. (Ch. 14)

A flirtation develops on Lady Grace's repeated visits to his office. Radnor is moved to a vague shame when he realizes that not every manifestation of nature need be admirable; on the contrary, "here she was, and not desired, almost detested! Nature detested!" Unfortunately, at this point Meredith turns away with a truism: the active intelligence must control nature, which "is a splendid power for as long as we confine her between the banks: but she has a passion to discover cracks; and if we give her headway, she will find one, and drive at it, and be through, uproarious in her primitive licentiousness, unless we labour body and soul like Dutchmen at the dam" (Ch. 36).

Meredith's frank analysis of sexual relations is more frequently traced to his poetic sequence "Modern Love" than to his later novels. The fifty poems which are not quite sonnets mingle incisiveness with compassion in a way which appeals to readers more than a hundred years later. But it is important to discriminate the achievement of "Modern Love" from that of the novels in their treatment of love. The novelist soberly tries to rebuild a world in which, one acknowledges, love does not last; the poet infuses a note of regret into his most cynical stanzas. Poem XXIX, for example, which declares that

> A kiss is but a kiss now! And no wave
> Of a great flood that whirls me to the sea.
> But, as you will! We'll sit contentedly,
> And eat our pot of honey on the grave,

offers a poignant backdrop to Radnor's mundane flirtation. Succinctness in the poetry contrasts with controlled elaboration in the novels. However closely or otherwise one may associate the facts of Meredith's own unfortunate marriage with the genesis of the poetic sequence (which after all was first published as far back as 1862), the novels after *The Egoist* are the work of a more settled although still razor-sharp intellect. By the end of his career Meredith had brought the real details of sexual relationships into an important place within the fortifications of the English novel, but we need still to go to "Modern Love" in order to appreciate Meredith's enduring sadness at what had been lost. The sense of the death of romantic love which hovers over the entire sequence is caught with especially stark beauty and power in Poem XLVII:

> We saw the swallows gathering in the sky,
> And in the osier-isle we heard their noise.
> We had not to look back on summer joys,
> Or forward to a summer of bright dye:
> But in the largeness of the evening earth
> Our spirits grew as we went side by side.
> The hour became her husband and my bride.
> Love that had robbed us so, thus blessed our dearth!
> The pilgrims of the year waxed very loud
> In multitudinous chatterings, as the flood
> Full brown came from the West, and like pale blood
> Expanded to the upper crimson cloud.
> Love that had robbed us of immortal things,
> This little moment mercifully gave
> Where I have seen across the twilight wave,
> The swan sail with her young beneath her wings.

II

Many other innovations in Meredith's literary method were closely related to women's liberation. He sought to depict an atmosphere of moral reality that would take full and intricate account of the perplexing world of manners, commerce, and democratic issues. That is the best mark of his Victorianism, which was constructive and forward-looking, and limited only by the inability, common to all ages, to project himself entirely out of his own age. Still his success is remarkable, his temper recognizably modern since he acknowledged the continuing possibility of fresh standards of conduct which could serve as a better guide to the moral life. What is interesting in *The Egoist* and in *One of Our Conquerors* is that the women characters are absorbed by the challenge to discover these standards, but not the men—who fail to realize how intimately they themselves are affected. Insensitivity, in this respect, leads to the defeat of Sir Willoughby Patterne by the very complex of social relations he relies upon for his status. The effort to sidestep the issue by Victor Radnor in *One of Our Conquerors* culminates in schizophrenia, no less. Here, Meredith was at the very base of the secular morality he sought to define. *The Egoist* represents his greatest success with this theme, *One of Our Conquerors* his most magnificent failure.

Meredith's heroines are placed in situations which threaten to compromise their reputations in terms of the existing conventions. They are confronted by crisis points in the relations between the sexes—breaking off a betrothal, divorce, remarriage, and extramarital union. Unlike some of his other famous contemporaries, Meredith accepted the ending of a love, and also the recurring growths of new ones, as ordinary, inevitable facts of life. Nevil Beauchamp (*Beauchamp's Career,* 1876) woos two women, is half-wooed by a third, before marrying a fourth. Diana Warwick (*Diana of the Crossways*) divorces her husband and marries again. The admirable Vernon Whitford (*The Egoist*) has had a previous unsuccessful marriage, a fact which startles Clara Middleton for only a moment. Nataly Dreighton (*One of Our Conquerors*) forms an extramarital union with a man whose wife will not divorce him; at the opening of this novel, there is a grown-up daughter from this union.

These departures from existing norms were not per se either right or wrong: the judgment and understanding with which they were made and maintained mattered most. Women—like men—had to rely not only on intellect but on an intuitive sense to guide them about right action. If they stubbornly insisted on acting solely according to emancipationist ideals (or any other ideals, for that matter), they, too, were egoists—vulgar, unfeminine, and unrealistic. Part of the attractive reality of Clara Middleton is that even when desperate she has this perspective on herself in her schemes to be free of Willoughby Patterne. "I have latterly become an Egoist," she admits, "thinking of no one but myself, scheming to make use of every soul I meet" (*The Egoist,* Ch. 16). Rebellion satisfied only the need of the individual rebel. The assertion of her ideals would produce no change in society, nor obtain any permanence in its enduring reality. The ideals would be smothered or mutilated unless she accepted the responsibility to establish vital interrelations between her act of defiance and the social structure, so as to alter it with originality from within. To convey the intricate reality of moral pressures besetting especially women pioneers of a secular morality,

Meredith employed a technique of scene arrangement where important changes in narrative or character took place offstage, as it were. At the same time his laconic style amounts to a refusal to explicate his meaning fully. He is the first novelist to rely extensively on such methods of deliberately withheld or obscured meaning, but he was not by any means wholly successful with them.

His best success was in the representation of Clara Middleton's dilemma in *The Egoist*. Clara had simply and only to break off her engagement, perhaps no very great thing, but largely as a result of Meredith's technique a wealth of implication surrounds this decision, showing that the dispute between her and Willoughby Patterne was "between a conventional idea of obligation and an injury to her nature" (Ch. 30), and emphasizing also that the dispute was not resolved, from the woman's point of view, simply by running away from Patterne. This is one of the important successes of *The Egoist*. The independent woman "feels" her way toward responsible action, realizing that the solution to her problem is not obvious but complicated, and further, that the onus is on her to seek the solution. Mrs. Mountstuart Jenkinson's epigrammatic flair, which turns Clara into "a dainty rogue in porcelain," serves primarily to convey this. Mrs. Jenkinson's exchanges with Willoughby are frequently prose conceits intended to be grasped without being dissected. Willoughby becomes a figure of fun the more patiently he plods after their meaning. Yet the conceits have no real power because while sexual undertones were probably intended, they are not strong enough to generate creative tension.

The failure is aggravated in *Diana of the Crossways* (1885) to the point where artistry suffers. The novel addresses itself to more complicated issues than breaking off an engagement. Diana was to seek a divorce from her first husband, be involved in a Cabinet scandal, and remarry at the end. The real-life story of the Honourable Caroline Norton provided Meredith with most of the material he needed, and suggested the kind of "flecked heroine of Reality" he wanted both feminists and society as a whole to understand. Mrs. Norton's life conveniently epitomized certain issues relating to female emancipation. It told of a beautiful and intelligent woman striking out into a male world and encountering situations that tested her tact, judgment, and good sense.[5] But Meredith's withheld meanings are nothing more than a failure of nerve. The quite extraordinary thing about this novel of divorce and remarriage is that the reader meets neither the husband, Warwick, nor the person Diana is accused of having an affair with, Lord Dannisburgh. On the other hand, a clear tactical emphasis is placed on Diana's beauty and intelligence, resulting in the creation of a character who answered to feminist aspirations, no doubt, but is otherwise fictionally implausible. Meredith's novel highlights tendencies that were becoming common in much popular fiction about women's rights and wrongs, but it is something of a literary curiosity now because the technique of succinctness and implication was overdone. By the standards of the 1880s, the story of a divorcee was a daring one, but Meredith's deference to his readers led him to produce what is virtually a dismembered novel. From a literary point of view, its highly enthusiastic reception at the time of its appearance might be explained by what its readers, prepared by emancipationist discussions pursued endlessly, filled into the gaps of the actual novel they read. Meredith himself believed that in Diana Warwick he had created a portrait which was both convincing and psychologically true.[6] W. E. Henley, praising his style, declared that "every touch [was] to the purpose, and every sentence packed with significance and luminous with weight."[7]

In *One of Our Conquerors* Meredith dealt with the more difficult theme of a free union with much greater conviction, bringing a degree of sophistication to his literary method which fascinates students of the novel even today. Nataly Dreighton and Victor Radnor have lived in illegal union for twenty years, since his wife will not give him a divorce. They now have a daughter, Nesta, a nearly grown woman. In joining herself to Radnor, Nataly had not acted out of a self-conscious wish to "liberate" herself. She had no theories about women needing to have greater freedom of action; she simply followed the dictates of her heart. Circumstances and her character led her to act intelligently despite the cost. Of her decision to live with Radnor although he was still married she says,

> "At the vilest, I cannot regret my conduct—bear what I may. I can bear real pain: what kills me is, the suspicion. And I feel it like a guilty wretch! And I do not feel the guilt! I should do the same again, on reflection. I do believe it saved him. I do; oh! I do, I do. I cannot expect my family to see with my eyes." (Ch. 11)

Nataly is oppressed, however, by the thought that she and Radnor must somehow rehabilitate themselves in society, or else in humility live obscurely. Radnor labors only under a sense of some slight social disadvantage. Egoistically he expects to be able to buy the social acceptance of his irregular union, or successfully gloss it. Two earlier attempts to install themselves as a respectable county family, at Craye Farm and then at Creckholt, have ended in failure. Nataly experiences deep misgivings at Radnor's insensitivity to their moral predicament. Now Radnor embarks upon his most ambitious gambit for acceptance of Nataly and himself—his Lakelands project, as a result of which Dudley Sowerby, a member of a wealthy county family, asks to be allowed to pay court to Radnor and Nataly's daughter Nesta.

It seems as if Radnor's power and money, by buying an entry into the aristocracy, will finally eradicate the social blot. Radnor increases the ostentation, until Nataly can ignore no longer her responsibility, long forgotten, to play a more active part in their fortunes: she decides to inform Sowerby of the nature of her union with Victor, and hence to confess to Nesta's illegitimacy. It is not simply a social point but a moral one as well, one which Meredith elucidates in his distinctive style:

> It came of her quick summary survey of him, which was unnoticed by the woman's present fiery mind as being new or strange in any way: simply it was a fact she now read; and it directed her to reproach herself for an abasement beneath his leadership, a blind subserviency and surrender of her faculties to his greater powers, such as no soul of a breathing body should yield to man: not to the highest, not to the Titan, not to the most Godlike of men. Under cloak, they demand it. They demand their bane. (Ch. 25)

Sowerby, informed, is stricken; his suit with Nesta falls through. Nataly is human enough to be overcome by the effort of this second great independent action. Both when she decided to live with Radnor and when she frustrated his scheme to gain an entry into the aristocracy, her responsibilities were clear and she fulfilled them with courage. Other responsibilities in the small change of life that directly followed these great efforts were more difficult to discover but still had to be fulfilled. The search for them saps Nataly's will to live and she dies.

In *One of Our Conquerors* Meredith imbeds in the social reality issues of sexual ethics arising out of women's liberation, and thereby discovers for us, in the major insight of the book, their relative power to influence change in society. An extreme diversity of implication and cross-implication places intangible limits on pioneers, witting or unwitting. The moral life is lived not only in the decisive points of one's career but in the intervals between as well. In the absence of clear guidelines, one has to rely heavily on an intuitive approach to seek out and fulfill one's responsibilities. Such an approach, owing to its elusiveness, may try one's moral stamina beyond endurance but it is ultimately productive of the sanest conduct and harmonious with the most constructive life processes.

Meredith's novels made him the one unqualified hero of the feminists of his time. As one who was "much at heart with them" he appreciated the kind of challenge faced by women who called into question long-standing conventions regarding their status and independence.[8] On the one hand, "through the contraction of their understandings caused by an exclusive devotion to maternity and domesticity," they were liable to react often impulsively and irrationally in circumstances requiring difficult ethical decisions.[9] On the other, a strong body of public opinion would "not only resolutely bar the fortress they [held] against feminine assailants, they [would] punish offenders sharply."[10] Women as free spirits had a precarious task in balancing independence with a fundamental sense of responsibility to society at large. Therefore they should cultivate powers of self-reliance and employ intellect to the full. They had to make an independent effort to help themselves, for this was the essence of freedom. "What with nature and the world, they are the most heavily burdened," Meredith admitted, but, he added, "I can foresee great and blessed changes for the race when they have achieved independence; for that must come of the exercise of their minds—the necessity for which is induced by their reliance on themselves for subsistence. Thus they will work out their problem."[11]

III

Meredith's lifelong interest in women's problems was matched by an incisive critique of egoism in men. His *Essay on Comedy* makes claims of the first magnitude on behalf of women: their status provides a touchstone of morality, indicates the stage of civilization of their society, and directly inspires a highly developed genre of literary activity. Remarkable authorial equilibrium saves these claims from either stridency or overearnestness; couched in elegant, unstrenuous language, they appeal to common sense, confirming Meredith as the apostle of the social man. In *Beauchamp's Career* (1876), Meredith had depicted man's political face in the egoistic maintenance or pursuit of power over his fellows at large; *The Egoist* (1879) is a close-up of this face, showing him in his relationship with one of his fellows. The novel is a brilliant analysis of what is now called male chauvinism.

Love binds a man and a woman in the commonest natural relationship and in the smallest significant social unit. "In other words, love is an affair of two, and is only for two that can be as quick, as constant in intercommunication as are the sun and earth, through the cloud or face to face" (*The Egoist*, Ch. 7). The lone individual, on the other hand, the primeval egoist, is the "original savage" (Ch. 11). Animal imagery is quite often used to score this ironically. Willoughby Patterne is at various times a hound, a tiger, an enormous bird of prey, a spider, an insect, and then simply a monster who would drag Clara "through the labyrinths of his penetralia." Combining the comic with the menacing, the imagery evaluates the protagonist unostentatiously from a moral point of view.

In its civilized form, egoism is now "a voracious aesthetic gluttony" (Ch. 11). Since its demands on the external world are fully met, it refines, exquisitely and insatiably, its demands within the individual. "This growing too fine is our way of relapsing upon barbarism," declares Dr. Middleton, Clara's father (Ch. 43). Willoughby relapses to the beast within him the more he pursues the satiation of his ego, and this must now be sought, since his social position is assured, in his most intimate relationship—with women. The imagery of the beast has obvious sexual connotations but again Meredith's excessive discretion forestalls a wholly successful creative tension between them and the novel's comic art. The "voracious aesthetic gluttony" is in fact the hidden libidinous drive which disguises itself in an absurd sentimentality which the women pursued by Willoughby instinctively fear.

Sentimentality is the language of self-love. In praising the beauty of the loved one, the egoist is praising himself for having secured it to himself. The unnatural tone of Willoughby's language sets Clara "vainly sounding for the source and drift of it" (Ch. 6). His sentimentality is not venial hyperbole but is indicative of a nature fundamentally out of tune with the world. In a recent essay, his self-love has been aptly characterized as "a form of self-copulation."[12] In the realm of manners, male egoism and its corollary sentimentality make the best use, for male benefit, of the existing conventions relating to the sexes. The more Willoughby's sentimental language refines, the further—by almost a natural law, this being Meredith's point—does it remove its object from the world and into the labyrinth of the monster. Such an object has then no rights as an individual, since sentimentality makes the man the woman's whole world; she has no existence outside his pleasure. He possesses her entirely, without any obligation in return. Women are saddled, as a result, with a code of lifelong fidelity, lifelong widowhood in honor of a dead husband, restriction of their role to copulation and maternity, and submission to men in every sphere. There is "an infinite grossness in the demand for purity infinite, spotless bloom" (Ch. 11). The refining of language produces, tragicomically, an opposite result—opaqueness which denies simple humanity to half of society.

Willoughby Patterne is not a completely individualized figure; we know him especially as the detailed ultimate development of a dominant trait in men. Meredith had said that men who were "overblown, affected, pretentious, bombastical, hypocritical, pedantic, fantastically delicate" were the proper objects of the Comic Spirit (*Essay on Comedy,* p. 89). Willoughby fits the description exactly. An exploration of the "finer essences" of egoism, its casuistries, its self-deception, and its ultimate sexual brutality drives home only the triviality of the love convention which sustains men in their dominance over women. This effect, precisely, is what is comic. "The laughter of Comedy," Meredith wrote, "is impersonal and of unrivalled politeness, nearer a smile; often no more than a smile. It laughs through the mind, for the mind directs it" (*Essay on Comedy,* p. 88).

The brilliant plotting of the novel is especially directed to trapping the male in his own snares. Willoughby becomes the instrument of his own fate. He has drawn Clara so close to his bosom that she revolts; contrary to his expectation, she gladly accepts his stipulation that she marry Vernon Whitford; and Laetitia, whose steadfast devotion he has repeatedly spurned, withholds it when he really needs it. Willoughby receives his just deserts, it is true, largely as a result of a kind of self-generating moral truth which comes to bear on all who violate justice in social relations.

But it was not simple retribution which Meredith was after. With *The Egoist* as sole evidence, it would have been easy for the insensitive to believe that only an absurd exception was being chastised. Meredith addressed himself to the further task of depicting the moral sense as forcibly invading the male mind, and denied by it thereafter only at the cost of personality disintegration. How a tangible idea of morality impinged on Victor Radnor's brain is a major theme of *One of Our Conquerors.* Radnor is a capitalist on an international scale. His acumen in using his wealth to bend society to his wishes has led him to believe that he has full control over his entire life. He is an egoist by virtue of his financial genius, just as Willoughby Patterne is one by virtue of his class. Like Patterne he is eventually compelled to realize that his power avails him little because he has ignored the moral issues involved in his relations with women. The practical, materialist money-maker, another egoistic demigod of the times, is brought "by hard degrees to conceive it to be the Impalpable which has prevailing weight" (*One of Our Conquerors,* Ch. 13); his entire being is physically defeated by the moral consciousness whose existence within himself he denied.

Of the "Impalpable" Meredith gives his protagonist an "Idea" at the outset—in a typically ludicrous collision with concrete fact: Radnor slides on some discarded fruit peel and falls flat. An altercation arises with the working man who helps him up, and who, offended by Radnor's condescending manner, tells him to drop his "damn punctilio" (Ch. 1). In Radnor's mind the word "punctilio" becomes inextricably associated with his fall. Not perhaps till the end of the novel does the reader realize that this incident actually marks the onset of a slow inevitable process of mental derangement, a direct illustration of Meredith's conception of the comic which "refines even to pain."[13] The fall causes a lesion on his brain just as "punctilio" causes a metaphorical lesion in his egoistic thinking:

> He tried a suspension of his mental efforts, and the word was like the clapper of a disorderly bell, striking through him, with reverberations, in the form of interrogations, as to how he, of all men living, could by any chance have got into a wrangle, in a thoroughfare, on London Bridge, of all places in the world!— he, so popular, renowned for his affability, his amiability; having no dislike to common dirty dogs, entirely the reverse, liking them and doing his best for them: and accustomed to receive their applause. And in what way had he offered a hint to bring on him the charge of punctilio? (Ch. 1)

Thus the accident and the word are inseparably bound with the encounter with an anonymous member of the poorer classes, a sector of society whose existence he had hitherto ignored.

The brilliant beginning of Chapter 1, sweeping from comic to serious, gives us a penetrating insight into the chauvinism of Radnor's mentality. He has collided not only with a section of society he is contemptuous of, but also with the moral reality whose existence he has never conceded. Meredith depicts the concept as struggling to rise to Radnor's conscious mind, and he cleverly overlays it with a rambling quality of thought proceeding partly by a species of reasoning, but also by association, much as it really would in a person's mind. The method has affinities with that of James Joyce of whom he is, technically at any rate, a clear precursor.[14] From the moment of its lodgment, the moral conscience besieges Radnor, importuning conscious recognition. He tries to articulate, and thus acknowledge, its intimations, but succeeds only partially. His plan for Lakelands, his ensnarement of Sowerby, his ostentation as a substitute for moral integrity, all these render him gradually less capable of bearing the presence of the moral "Idea" in his mind with equanimity. As Nataly aptly says, "He cannot take the soundings of the things he does" (Ch. 30). He will not countenance its presence willingly, because it will take the heart out of his ego, and thereby destroy his public life and power.

In the end he plans to stand for Parliament, intending to interpret his election as an endorsement of his illegal union with Nataly. Because he thus shows that he does not realize the true nature of the moral complexity arising out of his relations with the three women in his life, he fails to benefit from his successive intimations of the moral reality. The conflict of impalpable "Idea" with ego intensifies. He loses much of his rapport with Nataly, and when he learns of her death on the night of his election meeting, he suffers a schizophrenic attack. The derangement, begun with a ludicrous fall in the market place, is now complete. Radnor babbles to Sowerby about the Idea, "begging of [him] to listen without any punctilio (putting a vulgar oath before it)" (Ch. 42). Death soon follows. Through Radnor's mental odyssey Meredith placed the condition of women in the forefront of problems confronting society. Society's stalwarts will be brought low by the very complacency with which they regarded their private relationships with women.

IV

One of Our Conquerors is the product of a diverse and well-balanced social imagination, including but extending beyond the moral challenge of women's liberation. Meredith's idea of morality is of the dynamic kind. While the passing of moral judgments on characters, fictional or otherwise, was unimportant—like Vernon Whitford he would have said, "We'll leave severity to the historian, who is bound to be a professional moralist and put pleas of human nature out of the scales" (*The Egoist,* Ch. 13)—discovering and acting upon one's responsibilities which arise out of intricate involvement in a milieu was task enough. The traditional assumptions of society, slanted in favor of men, made this even more a male obligation than a female one. It is futile to look for an explicit definition of morality. The moral sense is creative; its power to add value to human action resides, paradoxically, in its nebulousness. If reached for intuitively, it can be "surpassingly luminous, alive, a creation"; otherwise, it would have "the yellow skin of a Theory, bred, born of books" (*One of Our Conquerors,* Ch. 40). Its locus, the consciousness, is the principal quarry of the novelist. "Brainstuff is not lean stuff," Meredith wrote, "the brainstuff of fiction is internal history, and to suppose it dull is the profoundest of errors" (*Diana of the Crossways,* Ch. 1). *One of Our Conquerors* is an unalloyed testament to the secular sensibility. The novel's incoherence, for which Meredith has often been criticized, may be justified partly by the magnitude of the task he set himself—that of representing the elements, and frequently the detail, of a unified secular morality.

Most of the contemporary reviewers of *One of Our Conquerors* could speak of nothing but its style. The *Spectator* said that it was "a literary manner which even in these days of affectation and strain is of unique perversity."[15] Another review faulted the novel for incoherence, prolixity, straining after epigram, seeking after the uncommon, lack of firmness in character-drawing, and allusiveness.[16] Lionel Johnson alone related Meredith's style to his subject matter: "If the chief influences brought to bear upon the chief characters be influences of the great and busy world, and of crowded and complicated life, then the style reflects the nature of those influences." Not unexpectedly Johnson went on to write the novel's most perceptive critique. He declared, "It is not too much to say that 'the world' or 'society' or 'the public' or 'the nation' seems to rank among the *dramatis personae*."[17] Meredith had written, when he was just finishing the novel, that he was "a bit strained, as I have condemned myself both to a broad and a close observation of the modern world."[18] Since, in his view, reality resided in the interpretation of physical phenomena by the general human consciousness, the consciousness was what he sought to represent. He attempted to capture thoughts, ideas, and moods, principally. While wary about emotions, probably because of their direct physiological basis, he did not, as we have seen, entirely shirk their challenge. Even Meredith's best critics with the exception of Jack Lindsay have given no more than a cursory place to a close analysis of his style.[19] It will be a help to try to discover how far one can go in seeking a connection between the peculiarities of his language and his lifelong concern about the struggle of women for dignity and independence.

One of Our Conquerors depicts the general mind, the general consciousness obtaining in society, as some intangible but inescapable substance outside of which none of its people can subsist. The thoughts of any single person have a meaning chiefly as they represent a mode or convention of thinking. An accumulation of such thoughts can generate a sense of context. When the Reverend Septimus Barmby, having learned the facts of Nesta's illegitimate birth, proposes to her, confidently expecting to be accepted, Meredith represents Barmby's smug mentality in the following way:

> A vessel laden with merchandize, that has crossed wild seas for this particular port, is hardly to be debarred from discharging its goods on the quay by simple intimation of their not being wanted. We are precipitated both by the aim and the tedium of the lengthened voyage to insist that they be seen. We believe perforce in their temptingness; and should allurement fail, we fall back to the belief in our eloquence. An eloquence to expose the qualities they possess, is the testification in the promise of their excellence. She is to be induced by feeling to see it. We are asking a young lady for the precious gift of her hand. We respect her; and because of our continued respect, despite an obstruction, we have come to think we have a claim upon her gratitude; could she but be led to understand how different we are from some other men! (Ch. 33)

These are not really Barmby's conscious thoughts; they do not sketch an internal physiognomy. By remaining at a level of generality the language ironically recognizes the presence of a group in society which would understand Barmby and find his unspoken patronizing sentiments quite unexceptionable.

Similar methods are employed in presenting social occasions. As a typical instance, we may take the concert held at Lakelands, where the author attempts to suggest the social mood at one point through the abstraction chivalry:

Carriages were in flow for an hour: pedestrians formed a wavy coil. Judging by numbers, the entertainment was a success; would the hall contain them? Marvels were told of the hall. Every ticket entered and was enfolded; almost all had a seat. Chivalry stood. It is a breached abstraction, sacrificing voluntarily and genially to the Fair, for a restoring of the balance between the sexes, that the division of good things be rather in the fair ones' favour as they are to think: with the warning to them, that the establishment of their claim for equality puts an end to the priceless privileges of petticoats. Women must be mad, to provoke such a warning; and the majority of them submissively show their good sense. They send up an incense of perfumery, all the bouquets of the chemist commingled; most nourishing to the idea of woman in the nose of man. They are a forest foliage-rustle of silks and muslins, magic interweaving, or the mythology, if you prefer it. See, hear, smell, they are Juno, Venus, Hebe, to you. We must have poetry with them; otherwise they are better in the kitchen. Is there—but there is not; there is not present one of the chivalrous breeched who could prefer the shocking emancipated gristly female, which imposes propriety on our sensations and inner dreams, by petrifying in the tender bud of them. (Ch. 20)

Here, too, the atmosphere is not peculiar to the occasion alone. The general social attitude toward women that "hangs" in the air, as it were, is linked ironically to society's intangible reality. For instance, the odor of different perfumes in the concert hall, the chemist who provided them in the first place, the women who wear them, and the chivalrous males for whom the perfumes are a guarantee of ideal womanhood are all scanned in the single compressed sentence: "They send up an incense of perfumery, all the bouquets of the chemist commingled; most nourishing to the idea of woman in the nose of man." The stitching of subjects into one another in this way suggests that they are inextricable elements of the social fabric. The development of thought in this extract, though reasonable, expands and contracts and expands again the scope of its reference, giving an effect of ellipsis, of uncompleted meaning. Closer reading shows the impression of ellipsis to be illusory, although the structure of Meredith's meaning remains unconventional. An apparently cryptic sentence like "Woman must be mad, to provoke such a warning" is clarified when we realize that Meredith means emancipated women.

81

That he does not really condemn them may be seen from the ironical way in which he refers to the rather precious social ideal of the beautified, romanticized female: "See, hear, smell, they are Juno, Venus, Hebe, to you." Chivalry thrives on the unbridled fantasies men build around women. Emancipated women impose too much "propriety on our sensations and inner dreams," the novelist concedes sardonically.

The predominant feature of this style is its inordinate use of general observations, that is, of sentences referring to classes of persons. They can be of many kinds: "Chivalry stood"; "[Women] are a forest foliage-rustle of silks and muslins"; "We must have poetry with them; otherwise they are better in the kitchen"; "there is not one present of the chivalrous breeched who could prefer the shocking emancipated gristly female." Such general observations, it will be seen, are not really so difficult to explicate separately. But packed in paragraph after paragraph they give the reader an impression of impenetrable density and deprive his understanding of an anchor in particular detail. When some detail finally appears—it may be a speech of one of the characters, "Is Durandarte counted on?"—renewed efforts must be made to understand its relevance. (In fact, with this question about a soloist at the concert, Meredith brings a long dense passage, part of which has just been quoted, directly back to the occasion which provoked it.)

Like many radical experimenters, Meredith did not expect—or achieve—popular success. He declared,

> Innovators in any department have a tough struggle to get to the field through the hedge for a hearing. Mine has lasted about thirty-five years, and I still have only to appear for the bawlers to be in uproar. As I know the world I do not complain.[20]

His innovations of technique arose directly from an unfeigned response to the issues of his day. He resembles George Eliot in the way he restored women to a position of dignity in human affairs by relying upon an intricate philosophy adapted from evolutionary ideas. But where George Eliot was concerned mainly to show where remedial action was necessary in order to preserve the traditional code, Meredith made a considerable advance in ethical thinking in bypassing specifically Christian ethics and in treating moral issues as challenging in a profoundly creative, human sense. This was a boon to feminists in two ways. First, his approach ensured that the new freedom women sought would not be condemned out of hand. Clara

Middleton could break a betrothal, Diana Warwick could leave her husband and marry again, Nataly Dreighton could enter into a relationship with a man already married—such actions were not necessarily in themselves wrong, although a responsibility devolved upon these heroines to seek the most satisfactory adjustment with society at the same time. Second, Meredith traced a pattern in nature to show how the refusal of men like Willoughby Patterne and Victor Radnor to countenance original acts of defiance (Patterne found such acts unthinkable, Radnor regarded them as unimportant) brought retribution upon themselves.

Meredith stretched the possibilities of his literary experimentation to their uttermost in an effort to represent the subtlety of his conceptions of moral awareness in the individual. His comedies of manners discriminated incisively between ephemeral conventions and genuine moral substance and opened the way to a major redefinition of morality in human affairs, one which has a validity even now. That the main issues of women's liberation provided him with fundamental matter for his task exalted considerably the movement's status and importance. He showed how a contemporary issue could be interpreted in terms of its permanent underlying significance for human beings.

4 Moore: Realism, Art, and the Subjection of Women

George Moore's numerous, often conflicting allegiances—Graham Hough refers to them as a "pell-mell jumble of passions and revulsions"—discourage efforts to unify, through interpretation, a sensibility eclectic by nature. As a man, Moore delighted in women's company even as he remained convinced of their secondary status in regard to men. As a Realist after the manner of the French novelists, he dealt with the moral and economic straits into which women were unjustly thrust, with a tacit sympathy that could only have been the fruit of social understanding. As an early English representative of the Aesthetic movement, he saw women's efforts toward freedom, rather limitingly as is now evident, as the expression of an innate artistic faculty common to all human beings. These three broad facets of George Moore do not cohere easily, and to discover greater coherence between them than actually exists would falsify his variegated literary character. When projected onto the literary scene, they seem to mark off important fractures in the mirror of the late Victorian sensibility soon to disintegrate even further.

"Any account of him without reference to him as a lover might as well not be told," Joseph Hone observes.[1] Moore confessed with stylish offhandedness, "I loved women too much to give myself to one." He was quite enamored of the pose of the successful lover. He could be as witty about the hazards of his role as he could be "outrageous" about the role of women: they had "a better apprehension of love when in olden days they formed into processions and wound through flowery woods to hang garlands on Pan's enormous sexuality."[2] While it is admittedly difficult to distinguish between truth and invention in the autobiographies,[3] it is clear that Moore was not a true cynic, nor simply a philanderer. He was boyishly enthralled by the "womanliness" of woman, which evoked in him attitudes of chivalry and compassion. He could write with a grave sympathy about the death of a prostitute, or about the brutalizing drudgery of a maid-of-all-work.[4] According to Hone he was even touched by the idealism of the suffragettes.

For much of his life, Moore regarded women as eminently fit subjects for art, often giving the impression of being interested in them mainly for the sake of the end artistic product—whether on canvas or as a little cameo in prose. He frequently claimed that nothing really mattered to him but art, for it was superior to nature. "After five and twenty—certainly after thirty," he said, "love adventures are no longer indiscretions but matter for literary inventions." Hone records that in later life when Moore mentioned some episode with a woman, "he would usually say that he was now coming home to 'write an account of it for his new book.'" Moore never married. His wish to die childless apparently stemmed from a belief in Malthusian ideals—he wanted to avoid "the crime of bringing a being into the world," thereby augmenting an already rapidly increasing population.[5]

While he was always happier in the company of women than of men, he never held a brief for women's liberation, entertaining the traditional fear that they would be "unsexed" by it.[6] He remained convinced to the end of his days of their secondary status:

> Every woman knows deep down in her heart that all her existence is comprised in man's love of her, and that if we were to withdraw our love she would become instantly a thing half our size, with sloping shoulders and wide hips and usually short-legged. It is our love that clothes her in silk and fine cambric and adorns her with laces, our love puts bracelets upon her arms, ear-rings in her ears, pearls upon her neck and too frequently diamonds in her hair . . . and I think, too, that it ill becomes [women] to praise sexual virtue, which has cruelly enslaved them, turning them into kitchen maids, laundresses, nuns or wives.[7]

Of women's intelligence, of their capacity to develop their potentialities in the same way as men, Moore says not a word. These were democratic considerations, and Moore hated democracy as the enemy of art. He expresses his denial of equal status to women in much the same terms as might be used in some quarters even today:

> All things certainly I would say in favour of women, and all things do for a woman, all but one, I would not lie for a woman; and however needful they are in our lives, and how-

ever delightful their influence is, still a woman is a satellite and it is to her honour that she is not ashamed to be one, no more ashamed is she than the moon.[8]

There is a note of exhilaration in Moore's autobiographical writings, as if they were written in the first flush, so to speak, of a new-found freedom from prudery in sexual and literary matters. But there is also a note of sobriety when he discusses the years of his young manhood in France. In Chapter 10 of *Confessions of a Young Man,* for example, we need not suspect invention in his description of the sense of his cultural detribalization on returning to England. He speaks of "my knowledge or lack of knowledge of the two languages," French and English, quoting examples of his poems in both to illustrate a difficulty which he felt to be symptomatic, ultimately, of some deeper confusion.

I

The relevance of the French Realist tradition to the women's movement may not be immediately obvious. The use of deteriorating and, in the main, unsympathetic heroines in the most influential novels—Flaubert's *Madame Bovary* (1857), the Goncourts' *Germinie Lacerteux* (1865), Zola's *Thérèse Raquin* (1868), *L'Assommoir* (1877), and *Nana* (1878)—probably even did the cause actual harm, so far as they were known in England. Presented unflatteringly as adultresses, prostitutes, or drunkards, such heroines easily reinforced the ancient fiction of women as the center of evil.

The consequence was partly one of method—common to both Realists and Naturalists at the time. There were, of course, theoretical distinctions between the two schools. Flaubert emphasized the artist's responsibility to "order and shape what we have seen," while Zola presupposed a structure in the material observed and set down by the writer. The common interest in impartial documentation showed a world where women did in fact support lives as secondary beings, and where, if they sought to escape their status by either self-improvement or flight, they invariably failed for reasons which the technique of writing made clear. In the case of middle-class women, Zola believed that a rapid, romantic education and an arranged marriage led straight to the adultery of the bored young wife.[9] As for women from the lower social strata, the combination of social and economic circumstances all too frequently led them to prostitution.

Zola was an important early influence on Moore and although, typically, public repudiation followed within a few years, Moore never forgot the basic lessons of the master. His enthusiasm for Zola's novels may be gauged from letters he wrote between 1881 and 1883. He acknowledged his debt to Zola humbly and explicitly when he brought out his first novel, *A Modern Lover*. "The fact that my novel has been successful may interest you," he wrote, "for, as I have already told you, I owe you everything."[10] Two years later, in December 1885, *A Mummer's Wife* appeared, employing Zolaesque techniques, but showing at the same time that Moore had found his touch. Although the influence of Zola persisted in *Muslin* (1886) and *Esther Waters* (1894), Moore's choice of theme, his settings, and his style were no longer entirely derivative.

Moore had once hoped that his novels together would make up "a small sort of *comédie humaine*."[11] If he is no Balzac, he nevertheless learned from Balzac and Zola the value of a systematic and unprejudiced scrutiny, in separate novels, of people of different classes. Because his women characters cover the spectrum of English society from working class to upper middle class, they represent as an ensemble the most comprehensive response by an English novelist of the period to the issue of women's freedom. The limited success of their careers at different levels stands as a corrective to feminist generalizations. Environmental causes of differing kinds prevented women from achieving a full-fledged development of their personalities. Moore's novels do not offer solutions for their predicaments. The reason, no doubt, is that he firmly believed solutions to be outside the novelist's province; the nonpartisan illustration of the predicaments was contribution enough. Yet while at the lower and middle levels his observation rings true, the limits of his own abilities as a novelist became increasingly evident as he moved to heroines higher in the social scale.

Even simply on a narrative level, *Esther Waters* (1894) is divisible into two roughly equal halves. Up to the end of Chapter 22 (there are forty-six chapters) the structure of Esther's milieu and the purely physiological factors in her nature loom larger than the element of her personal responsibility as determining agents of her conduct. The "strong bull-necked servant girl," as the *Spectator* of 2 June 1894 called her, submits to unrelenting social, environmental, and instinctual pressures beyond her ken, and beyond her powers of manipulation. The unequal nature of her struggle is peculiarly determined by the fact of her sex. In the second half of the novel, these pressures appear to recede, to the extent that Esther, reconciled with her seducer, pursues a life where individual decisions play a more significant part in her fortunes. This part is highly interesting for its picaresque episodes, but is notably different in tone.

Given the crucial seduction episode, we may describe the first half of the novel as self-generating. Esther's pregnancy, the birth of her child, and the struggle to maintain the child inevitably follow. Moore presented these stages of his heroine's life with a frankness and authenticity unprecedented in English fiction. Readers were convinced that the essential principles of Realism had at last been successfully combined with artistry in an English novel. A method of carefully proportioned emphasis serves as the chief controlling device of the novel. Variations in episode length combine subtly with skilfully selected realistic detail. For example, the actual seduction takes only a few lines to recount (Ch. 11). By contrast, the emotional effects of Esther's pregnancy and the effect upon her economic circumstances are spread over four chapters (12–15). The account of Esther in childbirth (Ch. 16) is followed by four chapters dealing with her struggle to maintain her child (Chs. 18–21). Moore's controlling emphasis does not violate the sequence of his narrative in real time. Each phase—seduction, pregnancy, birth, and economic struggle—is given attention proportionate to its duration in time and immediacy of sensory impact. Conventional ideas of a woman's guilt stand in abeyance when confronted by the real movement of life.

While Esther's narrative bore itself along up to the point of her frantic struggles both to earn a living and to maintain her child, the question her creator now had to decide was what direction her fortunes should thenceforth take. The full weight of circumstance and social reality had brought the servant girl to the limits of her endurance; what should now follow? Moore had been aware of this dilemma from the very beginning. He had studied the original model, Emma, "as one might an insect under a microscope" and exclaimed, "What an admirable book she would make, but what will the end be? if I only knew the end!"[12] The course that *Esther Waters* finally took indicates the nature of Moore's originality. According to Naturalistic practice the unequal battle of individual with environment invariably ended with the defeat of the individual; thus Esther should succumb, the pressure of social and instinctual phenomena should finally subvert her integrity, she should degenerate, that is, prostitute herself. Moore brings his heroine after much travail as wet-nurse and domestic servant right up to this point—but turns away (Ch. 21). This crucial episode where Esther refuses the solicitations of a young man in Leicester Square marks a turning point in the novel. Immediately afterwards she obtains a situation with a benevolent employer and her fortunes rapidly mend. Her rejection, not long after, of Fred for William, her old lover, represents the first prime example of her personal ability to choose without being hamstrung by external pressures. In her life thereafter as wife of a saloonkeeper, she is never again the complete victim of her surroundings.

The undeniable shift of emphasis does not necessarily indicate a conflict, or even a change of intention as is argued by Brian Nicholas in a recent essay on this novel. "The decor of the naturalist novel is there," Nicholas says, "[but] Moore no longer wants to face the full rigour of the naturalist equation."[13] From the very beginning of the novel we understand that Esther has a strong will and wholeheartedly subscribes to strict religious principles, as even Mrs. Barfield acknowledges (Ch. 12). She adapts—she does not abandon—these principles in extremity. Her escape from prostitution is consistent with her tough resilience. Besides, improved economic circumstances enable her to choose the man she wants to marry; and the marriage itself opens to her the comparatively greater freedom of the masculine world.

Up to this point her struggle illustrated factually the predominantly deterministic bias of the woman's world: her physiology rendered her vulnerable physically, and her subsequent lifelong responsibility for her child made her vulnerable economically, and in the eyes of society vulnerable morally as well. In terms of the duration in time which Moore skilfully employed, the man's guilt is momentary, something not seen, and therefore easily underestimated when not actually overlooked; the woman's guilt burdens her visibly ever after—unless she either abandons or destroys her child.

Once Esther marries William, however, she enhances appreciably the degree of autonomous action open to her. That is, she enters the man's world and obtains through it a measure of protection from gross economic and social pressures. The change is one of degree. At the level of the working class, men and women have to eke out an existence, but this difficulty the sexes suffer in common. In making book on horse races, William pins his ambitions on the only positive hope the poor have of escaping the constriction of their lives. When their friend Sarah Tucker is sentenced to jail William obtains a dim apprehension of the wider social structure that oppresses them:

> [He] was much exercised by his lordship's remarks on betting in public-houses, and his advice that the police should increase their vigilance and leave no means untried to uproot that which was the curse and the ruin of the lower classes. It was the old story—one law for the rich, another for the poor. William did not seek to probe the question any further, this examination seemed to him to have exhausted it; and he remembered that when he was caught he would be fined a hundred pounds, and probably lose his licence. And what would he do then? (Ch. 39)

In other words, Moore's novel expands gradually to reveal a concentrically oppressive milieu. In the inmost circle is the working-class woman; in the intermediate, the working class in general. Hemming them all around is an uncomprehending society irrelevant in terms of their need, but effectively curtailing their scope of free action. The story of Esther Waters served to remind readers of the more fundamental oppressions under which women of the lowest classes of society labored. Not least among its achievements, it demonstrated how a morally neutral observation of the realities of life could expose with ease the inadequacy of conventional religious principles when matched against strong, complex affirmations of life itself. It thereby helped to shatter the strongly held notion, already attacked by Hardy in *Tess of the D'Urbervilles,* that the loss of chastity in a woman necessarily deprived her of her dignity, integrity, and common rights as a human being.

The novel provides a perfect demonstration of how a writer's care for his art could, without explicit pleas or theses, affect tangibly the society for which it was written. After its publication many cases were ventilated in the newspapers of young women "compelled by the hostile attitude of society to destroy their illegitimate babies," and Moore was especially proud, Hone tells us, of the establishment of the Fallowfield Corner Home for Homeless Children by a reader who had been moved by the description of Esther's struggles as an unmarried mother. Moore's art did more: it also defined the boundaries of development of working-class women in general. The bounds on Esther's improvement in particular are pathetic. At the beginning of the novel, she arrives at the house of her first employer with a trunk full of books including *Lamb's Tales from Shakespeare.* Even that hopeful world of the imagination remains permanently locked away from her. The books are stolen by the time she is reunited with her old employer.

Kate Ede, the heroine of *A Mummer's Wife* (1885), belongs to the lower middle class, a higher social register than Esther's. She has been resembled to Emma Bovary, to Isabel Sleaford of Miss Braddon's *The Doctor's Wife* (1864), and to various women in Zola's novels—which at the moment only gives us warrant for the truism that *A Mummer's Wife* is in the nineteenth-century Anglo-French Realist tradition initiated by Flaubert's *Madame Bovary*.[14] Clearly, with a literary figure like Moore, critics tracing influences face a difficult task, perhaps ultimately unresolvable. Moore can be left with something to call his own. *A Mummer's Wife* captures sufficiently the atmosphere of a small town and the life and habits of English traveling actors for us to recognize the novel's original qualities equally with its derivative nature.

Kate is married to an asthmatic husband and finds herself hemmed in by household chores. In snatched intervals of rest she indulges in fantasies similar to those of the Realist heroines of novels of the time, especially to those of her prototype, Emma Bovary. But they are not essentially the same kind of thing. Flaubert's heroine, the supreme fantasist, "remains absorbed in romantic intention while fairly rolling in the dust," as Henry James says.[15] Kate's dreams—Moore frequently refers to them as "reveries"—differ very little from the quite ordinary desire to escape a life of monotony. Emma Bovary has time on her hands, and her fantasies are largely gratuitous. The evidence of Kate's kinship to Emma, undeniably present in Chapters 3 and 7, can be read too literally as an uncritical use of sources by Moore. Following Flaubert's example in *Madame Bovary* and *L'Éducation Sentimentale,* he undoubtedly had hopes of thrusting "a dagger into the heart of the sentimental school"[16] but—by their lesser intensity and shorter duration, and chiefly by the material way in which they arise out of context—Kate's sentimental leanings serve chiefly to illustrate the limited sensibility of a lower-middle-class woman.

Kate's "vivid interest" in fairies and goblins and her love of stories of "singular subterranean combats, of high castles, prisoners, hair-breadth escapes" do not constitute, one might think, a serious moral failing in a child (Ch. 3). Similarly, her taste for reading romantic love stories, "the second period of her sentimental education," reveals primarily the quality of her imaginative activity, aesthetically poor, perhaps, but not necessarily evidence of an inherently degenerate nature. Her moods are pauses for rest, naturally intervening intervals in which to simplify for a moment the complex facts of her existence. When Dick Lennox, the lodger, appears on the scene, she inevitably accepts him as her lover; her subsequent flight with him is an attempt to get out of the rut she has found herself in with her husband. The vicissitudes of her life with Lennox, at least up to the start of the decline in the fortunes of the traveling company, relate mainly to the petty human ways in which her expectations fall short of reality. Still Kate adapts herself to her new life so well that she justifies by both voice and acting ability the confidence of the company in casting her in a lead role. If fantasy has been instrumental in causing Kate to desert her husband, she re-establishes to a considerable extent a proper hold upon the new circumstances of her life. Her step is further justified in that Lennox marries her (Rodolphe Boulanger simply abandons Emma Bovary), and for a while at least she is reasonably happy.

In the second half of the novel, Kate becomes restless soon after her success as an actress. Her hitherto dormant religious instinct, which is little more than a strong prejudice, and her jealousy, given rein by Lennox's easygoing manner with women, undermine the possibility of a lasting sense of security in her new life. Drink proves to be effective in assuaging both guilt and anxiety. When joined to the straitened circumstances in which she and Lennox live after the failure of the company, it brings Kate to the real end of her resources.

Obviously this was how Moore hoped to graft upon the theme of lower-middle-class escapist dreams, the drink theme he had seen so extensively treated in Zola's *L'Assommoir* (1877). A claim on behalf of Moore's originality does not, however, overcome successfully this use of a second major source for a single novel. Moore presents Kate's alcoholism with entire conviction, yet the book does not recover from the resulting shift of emphasis. The woman who has fled to freedom degenerates not really on account of her moral incapacity, but on account of a factor introduced mostly as an "experiment" in the Zola manner, and given patently separate thematic treatment late in the novel. Essentially, the second half of the book consists of scenes of Kate's progressively increasing drunkenness, ending in the climactic violence of Chapters 26 and 27 which, as vividly realized episodes of this kind, had probably no equal in English fiction up to then. Nevertheless, there is consistency in the Naturalistic presentation of Kate's narrow sensibility. Motherhood marks for her the high point of her limitedly fruitful "dream" states. The unaccustomed deeper satisfaction which she experiences turns out to be, with a curious kind of irony, also a confirmation of the limits of her sensibility:

> it was pleasant [Kate found] to lie in the covertures, and suffer her thoughts to rise out of unconsciousness or sink back into it without an effort. And these twilight trances flowed impercep- tibly into another period, when with coming strength a feverish love awoke in her for the little baby girl who lay sleeping by her side. And for hours in the reposing obscurity of the drawn curtains mother and child would remain hushed in one long warm embrace. To see, to feel, this little life moving against her side was enough. She didn't look into the future, nor did she think of what fate the years held in store for her daughter, but content, lost in emotive contemplation, she watched the blind movements of hands and the vague staring of eyes. (Ch. 23)

Kate Ede is an intriguing heroine, a portrait which falls short of the first excellence because Moore, while he had learned the value of his sources, had not yet fully dissociated himself from them. To label *A Mummer's Wife* a Zolaesque novel is to recognize where both its achievement and its limitations lie. It transplants successfully a method of careful observation of human behavior, but it retains a thematic contact with its sources too close to allow unanimity about its original qualities. Kate's career illustrates the limits of a lower-middle-class woman's capacity to increase the individual comfort, meaning, and interest of her life. Her bourgeois upbringing, her limited intelligence, her ultimate inability to live out her defiance of moral rules to which she has long been habituated, these factors necessarily define the quality and nature of her search for freedom. With Kate this search amounts ultimately to a pursuit of a more satisfying emotional relationship with a man. She finds it in Lennox, and realizes that she has found it. If she loses it again, the fault is not hers alone; other factors in her environment—and faults in the literary method—eventually defeat her.

In the portrayal of the three middle-class women characters of *Muslin* (1886), Moore came completely into his own as a novelist interested in the real condition of women. He used but was no longer mastered by his "influences," applying them with originality to material drawn from his Anglo-Irish background. Thirty years after *Muslin*'s first appearance Moore himself evinced gratified sur-

93

prise at his having written truer than he knew: since he had never taken the slightest interest in social movements, he implied, it really was "a fine thing for a young man of thirty to choose the subject instinctively that Ibsen had chosen a few years before." He thought it strange that the critics of the eighties had failed to notice the similarity of theme between *A Drama in Muslin,* as the novel was originally called, and *A Doll's House. Muslin* is perhaps too exactly proportioned to be classed as a major novel. It has no vibrancy, no resonance to excite the imagination. Yet its symmetry, its restraint, its lack of ambitiousness, raise it well above the common run of novels of the time. The three main women characters stand in contrast to one another as representative types of womanhood. Cecilia Cullen, the embittered feminist, is at one end of the scale; Olive Barton, who is oblivious to everything and everyone save her own beauty and the husband she hopes to catch at the Dublin ball, is at the other. In the center is Alice Barton, who comes to understand the insult that is offered to her sex by the practice of rearing young girls for the sole purpose of selling them in marriage to the highest bidder. A new sense of self-respect grows in Alice, a greater awareness of the need for the independent ordering of her life. She puts a small literary talent to journalistic use, and she sensibly accepts a worthy doctor's proposal, despite her mother's withering contempt for the "meanness" of the match.

Alice Barton embodies Moore's views of the proper place of the sex in its relation to emancipationist ideas. "Higher than Alice no woman could go; any higher advance must be attended by unwillingness to accept the double duties of life," he said. By the double duties he presumably meant the exercise of intelligence and spirit, and the fulfillment of a sexual relationship with a man. If she sought to rely solely on intelligence and spirit, she would be denying the essence of her personality, which was inseparable from her sexual function. He emphasized this point in his criticism of Ibsen, who, he claimed, had substituted "an educational motive for a carnal one" in *A Doll's House.* From the standpoint of Naturalistic theory he held that nothing in Nora's character prepares us for her decision to leave her husband. "In the space of three minutes," Moore said,

> Nora, who has been her husband's sensual toy, and has taken pleasure in being that, and only that, leaves her husband and her children, as he has said, for school books. A more arbitrary piece of stagecraft was never devised.[17]

94

But in real life, too, Moore believed that the radical woman who broke out on her own to proclaim in public the rights of her sex ultimately did harm to herself, a point he illustrated in the character of Alice's close friend, Cecilia Cullen.

Cecilia's physical deformity reflects a distortion of her inner nature. Her lesbianism and her hatred for men mutually nourish each other. She also has a pathological aversion to sexual intercourse. She epitomizes the extremity of feeling to which some women were driven in their resentment against the weight of injustices borne by the sex. "I wish to save you," Cecilia tells Alice, "from what must be a life of misery, and, worse still, of degradation; for every man is a degradation when he approaches a woman" (Ch. 19). Moore makes excellent dramatic use of the warping in Cecilia's nature. In the same year that *Muslin* appeared, Henry James also studied, over the length of an entire novel, *The Bostonians,* the same kind of smoldering mentality in his portrait of Olive Chancellor. In Leo Tolstoy's *The Kreutzer Sonata,* a widely read short novel of the time, the central character, a man named Pozdnyshev, revealed a similar pathological aversion for sexual connections between men and women. Pozdnyshev reviles men for expecting their wives to submit to sexual intercourse after its primary function, childbearing, has been fulfilled. Through such demands, men made prostitutes of their wives, a view shared by even the progressive novelist Olive Schreiner. Pozdnyshev argues that since "of all the passions, the most powerful and vicious and obstinate is sexual, carnal love," new generations would certainly be forthcoming (Ch. 11). Therefore, "it doesn't take great wisdom to draw the same conclusion which animals draw—that continence is necessary" (Ch. 13), meaning not simply restraint, but an ideal for which to strive:

> "The highest genus of animals, man, in order to survive the conflict with other creatures, must band together like bees and not propagate irregularly; man must also, like the bees, nourish the sexless ones; in other words, man must struggle towards continence and never allow the kindling of carnal lust, to which the whole arrangement of our life is now directed." (Ch. 11)

True women's liberation would obtain "only when woman considers virginity as the noblest condition" (Ch. 14).

Unless we see the portrait of Cecilia Cullen (to say nothing of James's Olive Chancellor) against this general background of extreme opinion held by some people of both sexes, we may do feminists an injustice in interpreting the deviation in Cecilia's nature as peculiarly symptomatic of the female temperament. It is a major irony that no English novelist, except Moore (in "John Norton" and *The Brook Kerith*), cared to represent corresponding deviations in men although probably there was at least equal justification for such a theme.[17a] Moore regarded Alice Barton and Cecilia Cullen as "the efflorescence" of the moral atmosphere of the time, their natures "curiously representative" of "this last quarter of the nineteenth century" (*Muslin,* Ch. 19). Cecilia's feelings shock Alice, yet their basis in real feminine grievance renders her thoughtful; her insight into the indignities imposed upon her sex follows, and she regards with envy the comparatively greater freedom enjoyed by men.

Simply as a scrupulous account of the demeaning effects of social convention on well-brought-up young girls, this novel ranks high among minor works of emancipationist fiction in the period. But by interweaving a social background of poverty and unrest with the feminist theme in a progressive series of contrasts, Moore enhanced the merit of his novel. His technique of contrasts derives essentially from Flaubert, who in the famous scene of the Agricultural Show provided a telling contrast for the squalid wooing of Emma Bovary by Rodolphe Boulanger (*Madame Bovary,* Pt. 2, Ch. 8). In *Muslin,* Moore spreads and develops a series of contrasts over the entire novel with genuine literary skill, and—once the debt to Flaubert is acknowledged—even originality.

The two themes of "marriage market" and social unrest run at first side by side without comment. Moore repeatedly contrasts the worlds they represent, each time bringing the social theme to impinge more closely upon the unreality of the world of muslin. There are passages of concentrated brilliance in which irony is never far away. The clothes of the debutantes are compared to "armouries filled with the deep blue of midnight, with the faint tints of dawn, with strange flowers and birds, with moths, and moons and stars" (Ch. 16), but in the crush on the night of the ball the beautiful silks are hidden by the crowd and only exposed flesh—as at a market, no doubt Moore intended—remains visible. There is an ironic tolerance in the way this effect is conveyed:

> Only the shoulders remained, and, to appease their terrible
> ennui, the men gazed down the backs of the women's dresses.
> Shoulders were there, of all tints and shapes. Indeed it was like
> a vast rosary, alive with white, pink and cream-coloured

flowers; . . . Sweetly turned, adolescent shoulders, blush-white, smooth and even as the petals of a Marquise Mortemarle; the strong, commonly turned shoulders, abundant and free as the fresh rosy pink of the Anna Alinuff; the drooping white shoulders, full of falling contours as a pale Madame Lacharme; the chlorotic shoulders, deadly white, of the almost greenish shade that is found in a Princess Clementine; the pert, the dainty little shoulders, filled with warm pink shadows, pretty and compact as Countess Cécile de Chabrillant; the large heavy shoulders full of vulgar madder tints, coarse, strawberry-colour, enormous as a Paul Neron; clustering white shoulders, grouped like the blossoms of an Aimée Vibert Scandens. . . . (Ch. 17)

The parallelisms reach a climax in Chapter 13 when a deputation of peasants bargains with Mr. Barton outside his house for a reduction in the rents of their waterlogged farms, while Mrs. Barton conducts a financial transaction, basically similar, with Captain Hibbert, who wishes to marry her daughter Olive. Alice Barton and her husband show at the end of the novel that they have realized the social base on which they rest (Ch. 29). Olive, who does not, is forcibly reduced anyway to the peasant level she has never noticed. The belle of the ball who failed to secure a marquis, the season's catch, contracts a lung infection that obliterates her much-prized beauty. The description of Olive in her sickbed is noteworthy as a characteristic piece of Realistic writing, recalling Flaubert's unflinching observation of Emma Bovary's dying agonies:

[She] lay suffering in all the dire humility of the flesh. Hourly her breathing grew shorter and more hurried, her cough more frequent, and the expectoration that accompanied it darker and thicker in colour. The beautiful eyes were now turgid and dull, the lids hung heavily over a line of filmy blue, and a thick scaly layer of bloody tenacious mucus persistently accumulated and covered the tiny and once almost jewel-like teeth. (Ch. 26)

But at this stage the parallel worlds have converged to the point of revealing a humbling similarity between the life of elegance and the life of poverty in their susceptibility to identical misfortunes.

Muslin was hailed by the *Athenaeum* as "one of the ablest and most original novels of the year."[18] Moore was no longer a mere imitator; he had put the lessons of his masters to original use. His three women characters—while not, perhaps, completely flattering to liberationist aspirations—were closer to the social truths that mattered than most women's rights novels of the time, precisely because he placed his primary emphasis on the novelist's art. "Esther Waters is Alice Barton in another form," Moore said.[19] He might have included Kate Ede in this comment as well. His art tacitly defined boundaries from which they would never escape.

II

These novels give us an idea why the women's liberation movement failed to impress Moore. It presupposed a uniform ability in all women to understand and benefit from the claims made on their behalf. Its demands for rights and freer opportunities seemed largely to be made in a vacuum. Moore focused his attention not on the ideals of the movement, but on the claimants, and therefore on their relative capability to respond successfully to changes in their social and moral status. In *A Mummer's Wife, Muslin,* and *Esther Waters,* he offered an appraisal of the real condition of women in different classes of society. Since he did not treat his heroines as an idealist might, feminists saw no reason to regard him as an ally. Especially in his portraits of lower-class women, he showed the simplifications which feminism as a movement had to assume. More unpalatable than the hardship and injustice to which such women were subjected was the fact that their natures had received too strong an impress beforehand for them to benefit, to more than a small extent, from emancipationist objectives.

Moore was to show that this truth applied equally to women from the upper classes of society. Relieved of the stress of economic and social circumstances, such women had, correspondingly, a more sophisticated problem of sensibility in the context of emancipationist ideals. Quite simply it was a question of escape from a deep aesthetic boredom induced by conventional upbringing. Moore's upper-middle-class heroines set an escape process in motion by their response to art. The chief character in his novella, "Mildred Lawson" (in *Celibates,* 1895), wishes to be a painter, Evelyn Innes in a subsequent novel of the same name (1898) a singer. The search for freer self-expression in these art forms is an unwitting search for the life of passionate emotion—for which they are quite unprepared. Appalled at the revelation of their capacity for the life of the senses, they turn to religion, particularly the Catholic variety which with its ritual and mystique still bears the semblance of art. Moore shows, in other words, that art frees the imprisoned psyche only to present it with the dilemma of choosing between a frank surrender to sensuality or a return to an asceticism familiar through long habit. That Moore himself did not really find a way around these sharp alternatives any more than his heroines may have affected the art of both these later works.

The abnormality in Mildred Lawson's character stems from the same source as that of Cecilia Cullen. In his portrait of Cecilia Cullen in *Muslin,* Moore had represented the distortion which feelings of revulsion for sexuality produced in a few women. Although the social mores of the time did not go so far as to repudiate sexuality, they played a large part in instilling this repugnance by keeping young women in virtual ignorance of elementary human physiology. Largely through feminist pressure, however, the conspiracy of silence was breached; and the extent to which young women should be educated in matters of sex became a social issue in the nineties.[20]

Novelists made the topic a literary theme as well. Meredith made use of it in *One of Our Conquerors* when, with characteristic tact, he showed how Nesta, the daughter of Victor Radnor and Nataly, grew to a mature awareness of the complications which sexual knowledge and experience introduces into human relationships. Nesta learned in trying circumstances the true nature of her parents' marriage; and her friendship with a woman who has had a succession of affairs further advances her education. Henry James scrutinized the moral responsibilities and motives of adults in the sexual education of young women in *The Awkward Age* (1899). In his portrait of the heroine in "Mildred Lawson," Moore confined himself chiefly to examining the actual damage done to a woman's nature by the repressive education she received. The wells of feeling have dried up in Mildred Lawson so that, like Cecilia Cullen, she believes a woman can live a satisfying autonomous life quite independent of men. Only at the end does Mildred recognize how her arrested emotional development has cut her off entirely from any kind of deep experience.

Mildred seizes eagerly on the view of Mrs. Fargus, an avowed feminist, that "marriage is not the only mission for women."[21] Her motive in breaking off her engagement to Alfred Stanby echoes worthy feminist objectives: "She wished to live for something; she wished to accomplish something; what could she do? There was art. She would like to be an artist! She paused, astonished at the possibility" (Ch. 1). Enticed by art, she breaks the circle of her humdrum existence, and accepts with elation the new acquaintances she makes.

But a succession of peculiarly dry affairs with men, affairs she pursues without much enthusiasm, reveals disfigurements in her nature. In tracing the sterile involutions of Mildred's thought, Moore exposed the barrenness of the ideal of purity which was regarded as a woman's greatest virtue. The story deals with Mildred's mounting confusion as the criterion of chastity at all costs shows itself, not surprisingly, to be wholly inadequate as an exclusive guide to human conduct.

Mildred's celibate instinct, the absence of ordinary sensualism in her nature, prevents her from making a success either of art or of the invitations to committed living that her interest in art brings her. Ralph Hoskin, the painter who teaches her, dies withered by her inability to accept some untidiness in human relationships. Meeting his mistress, Ellen Gibbs, who is tending him in sickness, Mildred sees only that the "beauty" of their affair is lost, that, after all, "Ralph was not worthy of her" (Ch. 12). During her second affair Mildred begins to understand some of the quiet horror she causes, and she has an impulse to withdraw from a life emancipated in token only. "There's no heart left in me for anything," she confesses. "I wonder what will become of me. I often think I shall commit suicide. Or I might go into a convent" (Ch. 15). She is subject to various petty ailments, headaches, fainting fits, and generally run-down health—the usual marks of feminine neurosis. Then her lover's frank sexual advances shock her into fleeing the attachment, and she enters the Church of Rome, even pondering the further step of becoming a nun.

In thus switching from art to religion, Mildred has recourse to each pole of an interesting aesthetic dichotomy. Her interest in art had brought her, as art will, to confront life. Unable to bear life's reality, she withdraws into Catholicism, which seems to promise her the beautiful uncomplex life she sought but had not found in art. However, her interest in religion is half-hearted as well, and so, ironically, she returns to her original static position, her sensibility largely unaltered, her undeveloped character at rest at dead center between art and religion, since she is incapable of benefiting from either. At the end she cries, "Give me a passion for God or man, but give me a passion" (Ch. 22).

As a portrait of feminine aesthetic boredom "Mildred Lawson" recalls—though it cannot match—Ibsen's *Hedda Gabler*. One critic described Moore's heroine as "one of the most interesting and one of the most complex women I have ever met in fiction" and invoked Flaubert.[22] The detailed processes of Mildred's thoughts suggest the kind of violence which her upbringing has done to her sensibility. Liberation can have little meaning for such a woman, Moore seems to say, because society has effectively frozen her emotional potential. "Mildred Lawson" may have been inspired by a bitter disappointment in love, and Moore may well have had a private axe to grind in portraying a woman incapable of responding to love.[23] Yet the distance he maintained from his character remains impressive. It saved her from being the obvious vehicle of a private animosity, and showed her, instead, as an example of a conventional feminine mold which needed to be broken. Moore found this theme of sufficient interest to return to a more extensive development of it in *Evelyn Innes,* which appeared three years later.

The curious and confusing printing history of *Evelyn Innes* (1898) and Moore's varying opinions of the novel underline its standing as a literary curiosity, for no previous major novel in English had relied so thoroughly and extensively upon musical analysis and criticism to explain, directly and by analogy, the motivations of its central character.[24] *Evelyn Innes* appeared in the summer of 1898, having occupied three years in the writing. By autumn of the same year Moore had already revised the novel for the first time, sending Edouard Dujardin a copy "with all the corrections—that is to say, the text of the third edition."[25] Early criticism which Moore judged to be "hasty and malicious" had struck a chord of real uncertainty in him about the novel's worth. "I was next door to believing," he said, "that I had spent three years on the invention of an imbecility." His plans for dealing with Evelyn's odyssey were so expansive that the second part of her story, when she became a nun, appeared separately in 1901 under the title of *Sister Teresa.* With this volume he brought out a third version of *Evelyn Innes.* He now proclaimed the novel to be "one of the most powerful literary aphrodisiacs ever written." However, after an interval, he spent nearly a year on yet another revision. In January 1908 he told Dujardin, "I have rewritten the novel from top to bottom. Not a line of the original remains—yes there is the first sentence." In this version Evelyn decides she has no vocation for the religious life and becomes a social worker.

After the revision of 1908, according to Hone, Moore's opinion changed once again: it seemed to him, eventually, that the third edition of 1898 was the best. But when the first collected edition of his works was planned in America, Moore, assailed yet again by deep uncertainty, instructed that *Evelyn Innes* and two other novels "were not to be resuscitated." However, he apparently changed his mind again and the novel was among the twenty volumes when the edition was completed in 1924. The last stage of this confusing printing history relates to the Uniform Edition 1927–1933 and the so-called definitive Ebury Edition 1936–1937, from both of which *Evelyn Innes* is dropped. This suggests that at least with *Evelyn Innes* Moore did not primarily intend merely to add to the excitement of the book collector's game. He appears rather to have been genuinely unable to form a definite opinion of its worth. In the end, with different publishers owning different versions, his difficulties became well-nigh insoluble.

For the source of his uncertainty we must examine his elaborate, nearly convincing presentation of music as the staple of the imagination and a vivifying force that simultaneously mirrors and influences human conduct. In *Evelyn Innes* Moore makes practically the very last attempt of the nineteenth century to substantiate an influential belief among followers of the Art-for-Art's-Sake creed, that music is the one perfect unified art capable of evoking the most valuable response in human beings.[26] We recall that in his essay "The School of Giorgione," Walter Pater allowed that poetry, painting, and the other arts had unique elements untranslatable in any other form, yet he held that each, in striving to become a matter of pure perception, aspires toward the condition of music.[27] Having devoted much time and energy to producing a novel drenched in a musical atmosphere extensively developed upon such ideas, Moore seems to have alternated between fear that he might have produced a literary white elephant and elation that he had probably written a truly great imaginative novel. Moore's difficulties are, to a large extent, ours as well. By ordinary standards, *Evelyn Innes* is a finely wrought work tracing with care and deep understanding the course of a woman's search for emancipation of the spirit. Like most of Moore's other novels, it may not at first sight seem to have any emancipationist content; but that impression arises simply because Moore preferred to deal with characters rather than with issues, as we have seen. By interweaving a woman's independent ordering of her life with epical themes in Wagner's music, he sought to give her actions a kind of archetypal significance. Here lies the book's great interest, and ultimately, its crux.

Both her father and mother being musicians, Evelyn grows up in an atmosphere of great music. She has a voice and hopes to be an opera singer, but her upbringing keeps her, like Mildred Lawson, sedate and unadventurous at home. Then the worldly Sir Owen Asher acutely manipulates the springs of her emotion, intending to entice her to elope with him to Paris and further her career at the same time. He paints an ironical sketch of her prospects at home— she would be bound by unspoken rules to make a socially advantageous marriage, to a duke preferably and, assuming she won some success as a singer, a status no better than that of a musical instrument which her husband would guard "lest someone should walk off with his means of subsistence" (*Evelyn Innes,* Ch. 7). Seeing her mortified by this picture of carefully nurtured secondary existence, Asher now woos her with music:

> Evelyn lay back in a wicker chair thinking. He had said that life without love was a desert, and many times the conversation trembled on the edge of a personal avowal, and now he was playing love music out of "Tristan" on the harpsichord. The gnawing, creeping sensuality of the phrase brought little shudders to her flesh; all life seemed dissolved into a dim tremor and rustling of blood; vague colour floated into her eyes, and there were moments when she could hardly restrain herself from jumping to her feet and begging of him to stop. . . . He continued to speak of the motive of the love call, how it is interwoven with the hunting fanfare; when the fanfare dies in the twilight, how it is then heard in the dark loneliness of the garden. She heard him speak of the handkerchief motive, of thirty violins playing three notes in ever precipitated rhythm, until we feel that the world reels behind the woman, that only one thing exists for her—Tristan. A giddiness gathered in Evelyn's brain, and she fell back in her chair. . . . (Ch. 7)

Entranced by Asher's analysis of the music he is playing, she is swept into love—she accepts, albeit with qualms, her sexual emotions.

In using Wagner's music to illuminate the obscure logic of emotion, Moore was on safe ground by nineteenth-century musical standards. Wagner's epical dramas provided harmonious material with which to represent an æsthete's ideas of the emotional dialectic of the soul. It seems quite incredible that one with such an unremarkable knowledge of music as Moore should have carried off with conviction the transposition of precise musical ideas and themes into fiction. That he did not really have much of an ear for music, or any

103

extensive firsthand acquaintance with it, close relatives and friends testify. Edouard Dujardin probably summed the matter up when he said, "I don't think that he had an ear, and it always seemed to me that his interest in Wagner, on whom we had endless conversations, was mainly literary."[28] But this only serves to underline the sustained technical feat that clothed with assurance and an air of rightness the detailed musical commentaries and analyses. Yet that is all they amount to: a close look at the extract and at innumerable similar passages shows that we are being shortchanged. We are told—we do not grasp—that Evelyn's musical sense has merged with her emotional nature. Moore has no expert knowledge of human psychology, and his musical analyses fail to serve as a satisfactory substitute. He meant them to function as more than analogies or symbols relevant to Evelyn's career. The musical descriptions of the Wagnerian dramas were to enter powerfully into her blood and represent as well as illuminate the process of transformation of her personality. There is a fundamental confusion here between the formal emotion of art and ordinary human emotion.

Fleeing to Paris with Asher, Evelyn becomes his mistress and achieves success as a Wagnerian soprano. Thenceforth she accepts the meaning of her life in the terms that Isolde, Elizabeth, Brunnhilde, and other Wagnerian heroines saw theirs. Evelyn herself acquiesces wholeheartedly in these acts of identification. Ulick Dean, coming into her life at the height of her career, recognizes the impassioned vessel of experience she has become. Swept along on emotion, it is her turn to woo. "I want you," she tells him, "to go through Isolde's music with me" (Ch. 14). With two lovers, her moral standing becomes at last clear to her. She sees that hers will not be the common dilemma of choosing one of two men. She has seen two Tristans, and wants both. Art has awakened a sensuality in her which will not be satisfied. "Her face contracted in an expression of disgust at this glimpse of her inner nature which had been flashed upon her . . . and she turned her eyes from a vision of gradual decadence" (Ch. 21). Thus Moore has brought this heroine, as he did Mildred Lawson, to confront the moral problem which Victorians could only see as a pair of a mutually opposed alternatives, chastity or immorality. Neither Evelyn Innes nor her creator found a resolution to this dilemma.

In the last part of the novel Moore traces with the same quality of attention to musical inspiration the process of Evelyn's withdrawal from life. For example, she is reconciled to her father, conscious that she is acting a scene from *The Valkyrie:* "She knelt at her father's feet or at Wotan's feet—she could not distinguish; all limitations had been razed. She was *the* daughter at *the* father's feet. She knelt like the Magdalen" (Ch. 16, author's italics). The identification of art with reality is too pat. The novelist sacrifices the real examination of emotion in favor of one-to-one correspondences with art. Evelyn's aesthetic predecessors are John Norton of Moore's earlier novel *A Mere Accident* (1887), Des Esseintes (of J. K. Huysmans' *À Rebours*), Marius, and Dorian Gray. Like them she remains essentially an aesthete's creation carefully turned upon esoteric ideas of art but lacking full vitality or conviction.

Moore tells his heroine's story essentially as an adventure of the spirit, with a fine restraint, seeking out her emotional motives and presenting them without comment or criticism. The contrast between the opinionated young man of the *Confessions* and the author who here effaces himself so completely serves as further testimony of Moore's primary virtue as a novelist: from the very beginning he could maintain a highly effective distance between himself and the characters he created. Only the ambitiousness of his intentions in *Evelyn Innes* reveals the limitations of this skill. By means of a thoroughgoing use of Wagnerian themes and musical analysis, Moore sought to give a serious, detailed, and constructive account of the functioning of the moral sensibility in the context of emancipationist ideals. Artistic themes were to reflect, literally and exactly, human emotional processes. But despite prodigious efforts Moore does not succeed in lending conviction to the idea of the transcending emotional reality of art. Years later he was to say that the novel "rang false in my ear; too much brass in the orchestra."[29] Readers were more impressed by his labor than by his meaning, and this, largely, is likely to be the reaction nowadays. The *Athenaeum* commented, "He joins to great intelligence extraordinary laboriousness, which secures him the power of rarely making a mistake and as rarely enlightening by a flash of inspiration."[30] It may be that Moore himself recognized this as the novel's main drawback, and sought in his repeated revisions to capture the absent flash.

Moore's contribution to the issue of women's liberation was to offer a carefully discriminated account of the relevance of feminist issues to women at different levels of society. His characters issue no manifestoes, yet essentially they seek to free themselves from traditional constraints. The most significant comment which may be drawn from his work as a whole is that the quality of their idealistic longings is directly governed by the material, ethical, and environmental structure of their life in the world. His expository technique as a novelist remained true to the ideals of the French Realists even after he had won free from them. He never believed it to be the novelist's province to propagandize new ideals, whether inspired by women's liberation or by any other movement. His presentation of women in actual contexts permitted only a limited optimism: women who sought to free themselves must rest content with a modest happiness, still as secondary beings; or else, trapped in a dilemma ultimately aesthetic in quality, they must forever oscillate between unbridled sensuality and a wasting asceticism. Sometimes one senses in Moore's novels a note of patronizing sympathy; at others one suspects that his demonstration of actual limitations to which women were subject was inspired by a conviction of women's decided inferiority. As we have seen, most of what he does is internally right, but in ignoring, no doubt for "Realistic" reasons, the dynamism of social change he may have excluded too much from his novels. At any rate one is struck by his singular lack of interest in—or his inability to push through to—the widest meanings of the social and moral life.

5 Gissing's Studies in "Vulgarism": Aspects of His Antifeminism

In the present revival of interest in the Victorians and sympathy for them there has been no discussion of the undeniable hostile cast of Gissing's novelistic practice in the portrayal of women and women's issues. Because his novels, especially those of the nineties, draw very fully upon the contemporary scene, it has even been assumed that he was unambiguously sympathetic to feminist claims. "On this subject at least," declares his most recent biographer, Jacob Korg, "Gissing's opinions were clear, consistent, and uncompromising. An enemy of the Victorian myth of the inferiority of women, he believed firmly that women were the intellectual and spiritual equals of men."[1] In fact, the opposite view is more tenable; and the novelist's art was adversely affected as a consequence. Certainly Gissing wished to see women given a wider general education, and he was concerned about their opportunities for employment. The fate of the large number of women doomed to a single life, as the population ratio of women to men clearly showed, engaged his sympathies. He is also on record as suggesting, more daringly, that "the only way" of effecting lasting improvements in the status of women was "to go through a period of what many people will call sexual anarchy."[2] The letters, regrettably, do not elaborate this last point but his novels—*Denzil Quarrier* (1892), *The Odd Women* (1894), and *In the Year of Jubilee* (1895), notably—make it quite plain that he entertained the proposal only to dismiss it with a degree of shallow flippancy. Gissing is the only important novelist of the period whose approach to emancipation looks rather more like reasoned animosity toward the movement. This claim gains considerable weight when examined in relation to his dismay at the growing vulgarity of the society around him. That was the novelist's wider concern, and it is fairest to see the issue in its light.

It is never easy to separate the person from the author in Gissing's novels. The works embody a broad skepticism toward society in general which George Orwell labeled "close to being reactionary."[3] Gissing resented long and deeply his exclusion from the privileges of superior social status to which he felt he had a natural right by virtue of his education and intellectual qualities. Individual frustration, taken together with his disgust at the dilution of social and moral values on the wider scene, found a creative outlet in the impecunious intellectual hero who figures in almost every novel. These young men are the "unclassed," pacing restlessly on the outskirts of a society they have ceased to comprehend. They regard the movement for the liberation of women from a superior vantage point as emblematic of social decay. Perhaps by association, Gissing's heroines, seeking to free themselves from traditional restraints, reflect some of this wider restlessness as well. Gissing wrote, after all, about a class of miscellaneous people bewildered by their social and cultural displacement in a rapidly expanding society. That is the underlying general aim in all his novels which gives us pause. But his error was to depend on "vulgarism," as he called it, as the principal lens for focusing his concerns in the nineties. As we shall see, it proved to be an inferior prism, lending itself to the idiosyncrasies of his vision rather than correcting them. In the latter phase of his long career as a novelist it effectively aborted any promise of full greatness in his art.

I

Gissing's early intellectual affiliations, not, it would appear, held very profoundly, had been mostly abandoned soon after he embarked upon his career as a novelist. By the time he was twenty-five he had lost the inclination to relate his records of human experience to any of the broad imaginative theories then current, whether metaphysical, humanitarian, or socialist. In 1883 he told his brother, "Philosophy has done all it can for me, and now scarcely interests me any more,"[4] a sentiment echoed by Waymark in *The Unclassed* (Ch. 25), one of the many characters in the novels closely resembling the author. If there were any two larger motivations behind his work one was his personal ideal of a class system based on scholarly culture, and the other, his two disastrous marriages. Both factors affected incalculably his attitude to women, causing him to present them with quite remarkable disenchantment in his novels.

Gissing gave ample evidence, in the numerous distinctions and awards he won, of gathering potential for a distinguished academic career.[5] But long hours of lonely concentration on his studies did not help to make him sociable. "He did not know what would offend, and he did not know what would please. . . . He had no social nerve," said H. G. Wells.[6] Gissing was also sexually starved, a fact which he acknowledged with surprising frankness, considering the time in which he wrote. "Why isn't there a decent name for the agony men go through at that age?" asks a character in *The Whirlpool* rather pathetically. He echoed the author's memory of his own privation which led him to an attachment with a young prostitute named Marianne Helen Harrison. Except that it was an irregular union, that relationship, on Gissing's part at least, was an honorable one. He regarded "Nell," as he called her, as a victim of society, and sought to rehabilitate her. Not, it turned out, a rewarding task.

He possibly saw in the relationship a kind of perverse novelty related to muddled theories about art and misery. At any rate it is difficult to understand the quixotic act of theft he committed mainly for Nell's benefit, an act that ruined his career and led to a term of imprisonment.[7] Overwhelming loneliness may have led him to marry her after all, in spite of the totally discouraging evidence he had seen of her character. The marriage lasted, in effect, nearly three years, and Gissing reaped in poverty, desperation, and embarrassment a pitifully full quota of suffering and emotional pain.

Nell died in 1887, five years after they separated. A few years later, Gissing plunged deliberately into a second difficult marriage. He had by then become convinced that for him "marriage, in the best sense, is impossible, owing to my insufficient income," and he relinquished, with a sinking heart, his ideal of a refined marriage partner from the upper classes. He confessed to Eduard Bertz, "There is no *real* hope of my ever marrying any one of a better kind, no *real* hope whatever! I say it with the gravest conviction."[8] In the interval following his first wife's death, Gissing experienced acutely the loneliness and frustration that so often drove him to despair. Finding his position at last insupportable, he decided to "resume my old search for a decent work-girl who will come and live with me."[9] The working-class girl he did find stipulated marriage, however. Gissing was plainly ministering to his physical needs. He paid scant heed to most other considerations, and in spite of the rather unusual but constructive intervention of his friend Morley Roberts, Gissing could not be discouraged from a second unpromising match.[10] It took, in the event, its predictable toll of the author over seven unhappy years.

"A Lodger in Maze Pond," one of Gissing's short stories, reveals the surprising insight the author had into his own actions.[11] One disastrous marriage over, and on the threshold of a second marriage, Shergold, like his creator, perceives the unsuitability of his partner. A friend tries tactfully to distract Shergold from his set purpose, as Roberts had done in Gissing's case. The intervention is opportune, and allows the committed man a chance for second thoughts. However, Shergold, with a curious doggedness, deliberately embraces the prospect of a second stretch of marital unhappiness, even though he sees clearly the ultimately self-defeating quality of his action.

If he courted certain unhappiness in successive marriages for art's sake, Gissing achieved his aim. "Lamentable though the fact may be," said the *Times Literary Supplement,* "it is startlingly plain that it was only so long as his domestic misery endured that Gissing maintained the peculiar intensity of imagination that distinguishes his characteristic novels."[12] Gissing's actual relationships with women must also account in important ways for some of his unflatteringly harsh feminine portraits, notably Harriet Smales (*The Unclassed*), Clem Peckover (*The Nether World*), and Ada Peachey (*In the Year of Jubilee*). Even with more sympathetic heroines like Rhoda Nunn (*The Odd Women*) and Nancy Lord (*In the Year of Jubilee*), Gissing was, in general, cool rather than generous. The saga of his marriages also contributed to his disenchanted view of love:

> "Men marry without passion [Henry Shergold says]. Most of us have a very small circle for choice; the hazard of everyday life throws us into contact with this girl or that, and presently we begin to feel either that we have compromised ourselves, or that we might as well save trouble and settle down as soon as possible, and the girl at hand will do as well as another." (*The House of Cobwebs,* p. 258)

Gissing's distrust of the democratic changes taking place aggravated such attitudes nourished on his own marital unhappiness. While he genuinely wanted the lot of the poor to be improved, years of enforced intimacy with them had only aggravated his personal repugnance for them. "Without wishing to be harsh to these people," he declared, "you must recognise how utterly impossible close relations with them become . . . I fear they put me down for a prig, an upstart, an abominable aristocrat, but *que voulez-vous?*"[13] The provision of fresh and more widely spread opportunities for education and employment meant little difference, if any, to the concept of a graded community. "All classes will be elevated, but between higher and lower the distinction will remain."[14] This exceptional caution about fundamentals of social improvements stemmed from a fear of dilution in the quality of life and society, an apprehension which Gissing found increasingly confirmed. Education brought only "extending and deepening Vulgarity," he told Bertz. Convinced that "the gulf between the really refined and the masses" had widened and would widen still more, he fell back on his rather wishful concept of an intellectual aristocracy. He called it "an Aristocracy of mind and manners," which would not demean itself by contact with a society of deteriorating values.[15] The concept epitomized his recoil from a society in transition. It expressed his personal distrust of social movement in the mass. Used as a novelist's standpoint, and reflected in many of his central male characters, it produced a close and biased—though far from invalid—study of type figures in a changing civilization.

He regarded issues relating to the advancement of women in a similar light. He acknowledged feelingly—in a way which reminds us that he spoke from bitter personal experience—the effects upon woman of her depressed status. Comparing the average woman to "the average male idiot" he believed her condition could be redressed, in part at least, by education, not primarily to enable her to compete with men on equal terms, but for the greater well-being of society.[16] Again, the distinctions between higher and lower would remain. Throughout his life he did not deviate much from the opinion he formed in 1880:

> A girl's education should be of a very general and liberal character, adapted rather to expand the intelligence as a whole than to impart very thorough knowledge on any subject. General reading is what I should advise a girl to undertake; and that reading should certainly *not* lie in the direction of Higher Mathematics or Political Economy.[17]

The letters to his sisters are full of fatherly advice, consistent with these principles, about the reading and other pursuits they should be undertaking to improve their minds. He believed that the proper adoption of his counsels—he often detailed approaches to particular authors somewhat like a schoolmaster—would in truth emancipate their minds. In his letters to them he is strangely silent, however, on other topics relating to feminine emancipation, notably women's relations with men. Arthur C. Young rightly points out that Gissing's prescriptions in fact aimed at producing the kind of refined woman he always had as an ideal, too far above him socially to be approached with love.[18] Neither sister married.

References to reading, art, and learning serve for Gissing as significant pointers to the moral quality of his women characters. In *The Unclassed,* Waymark recommends Rossetti's poems to the refined Maud Enderby, who, in shrinking from love, wrongly perpetuates "the old antagonism" of flesh and spirit (Ch. 19). He also lends books to Ida Starr, the prostitute he has befriended, "to cultivate your mind" (Ch. 26). The author impresses Lilian Northway in our minds as an intelligent and meritorious specimen of womanhood when a visitor to the home where she lives as Denzil Quarrier's mistress perceives that "she had read diligently, and . . . the book with which she had been engaged when they entered was a Danish novel" (*Denzil Quarrier,* Ch. 3). Conversely, education not undertaken for its own sake signifies a lack of moral fiber: Jessica Morgan's betrayal of Nancy's secret about her child (*In the Year of Jubilee*) seems to follow in part naturally from what we know of her grim determination to pass examinations. In the same novel the Peachey household is especially detestable for its evidence of half-education in the form of "cheap miscellanies, penny novelettes and the like" which lie scattered about.

In the same way that his desire for the improvement of conditions for the lower social classes was governed by the conviction that the distinction between superior and inferior classes would still remain, so in his attitude to women Gissing never conceded, expressly or tacitly, that women should be or are the full moral and intellectual equals of men. Gissing's heroes, with their author's approval, patronize their women, assuming a natural superiority in all important matters. For example, having influenced Ida Starr, the prostitute, to undertake a long and onerous process of rehabilitation, Waymark would have her "capable of yet nobler ideas" before she can be worthy of his love. At the same time, thinking of Ida's contender for his affections, the refined Maud Enderby, he feels that "there was no height of his own thought whither she would not in time follow him." Waymark foreshadows many a subsequent Gissing hero in the pompous tone of his utterances and in his smug opinions. Waymark, Quarrier, Barfoot, Tarrant, Hilliard, and Rolfe all accept unquestioningly the premise that, on the whole, women fall short of men in intellectual and therefore in moral quality. In the recurrent theme in Gissing's novels, the marriage of a refined man to a girl of a lower

order, Frank Swinnerton observed, "The fault of stupidity is invariably the woman's, the fault of weak generosity the man's."[19]

Intellectual power and breadth of knowledge were the sole indica-
tors of superior moral worth. These were male virtues rather than
female, an assumption it was easy for Gissing to make since as yet far
fewer women than men received anything like a complete education.
Only at the end of a life finally mellowed by his association with
Gabrielle Fleury did Gissing recognize the fallacy of equating intellectual capacity exclusively with moral fiber. "Foolishly arrogant as I
was," he declared,

> I used to judge the worth of a person by his intellectual power
> and attainment. I could see no good where there was no logic,
> no charm where there was no learning. Now I think that one
> has to distinguish between two forms of intelligence, that of the
> brain, and that of the heart, and I have come to regard the
> second as by far the more important. I guard myself against
> saying that intelligence does not matter. . . . But assuredly the
> best people I have known were saved from folly not by the
> intellect but by the heart.[20]

But by then—1903—his score or more novels had already been
written.

II

Although women's liberation forms a more or less significant interest
in nearly every novel of Gissing's, the issue looms especially large in
those he wrote in the nineties. *Denzil Quarrier* (1892), *The Odd Women*
(1893), *In the Year of Jubilee* (1894), *Eve's Ransom* (1895), and *The
Whirlpool* (1897) deal centrally with women of middle- and lower-
middle-class backgrounds, a social group Gissing knew intimately;
while *The Unclassed* (1884), one of his best novels of the previous decade, showed the relevance of liberationist issues to the lower classes.

The Unclassed excels, in candidness and understanding, the few
previous attempts in Victorian fiction to portray a prostitute sympathetically. Gissing presented in Ida Starr one of the first English
heroines from whose life the reader could gain an insight into the
motives and circumstances that lead women of the lower classes into
prostitution. A contemporary critic described the novel as a tale of

lower-middle-class life in the manner of Zola.[21] The *Athenaeum* was sufficiently shocked to ask whether "the disagreeable subjects with which Mr. Gissing deals" were proper material for literature.[22] There appears to be little external documentary evidence of Zola's influence on Gissing. Early in his career the author told Frederic Harrison that he had never read Zola's work and that the qualities of his own writing resulted from his own reactions to the poor.[23] Later Gissing acknowledged that the continental writers—including, presumably, Zola—impressed him more than English ones. Like Zola, Gissing, too, sought authenticity at first hand. For instance, before writing *Thyrza* (1887), Gissing went to Lambeth, the working-class district in the south of London, where he spent many hours gathering material.[24] But the relationship of Gissing to Zola is better traced in the novels themselves, particularly the earliest ones. *The Unclassed* undeniably resembles characteristic novels of Zola in some points of subject-matter and technique.

Partly in the Realist manner, Gissing showed that among the poor the accumulation of petty circumstances helped to create an environment basically hostile to women. They were untrained for any but the most menial jobs. Those who rebelled against the drudgery or the humiliation or both could only choose prostitution as a way out of the rut. They were unfitted for any useful role. Ida Starr's story, recounted in Chapter 17, reads like a Realist novel in miniature, foreshadowing, especially in the unceasing harassment of the central figure, the more fully developed saga of the working-class woman in George Moore's *Esther Waters*.

The contrast to Ida Starr is the spiritualized Maud Enderby, undeniably the forerunner of Mildred Lawson and Evelyn Innes, George Moore's arid heroines. Maud's religious education has choked off her capacity for love, while her sheltered upbringing has made her insensitive to the poverty around her. Ida and Maud stand for the brothel and the hearth, identified by Ray Strachey as the two sectors of Victorian society linked by the surreptitious commerce of men. Waymark, Gissing's hero, demonstrates a more open and humane attitude toward both. In the process not just the prostitute but the cloistered ideal as well is shown to labor under disfigurements of character caused by prevailing social canons. Gissing displays a remarkable degree of penetration in his portrayal of these two women, revealing the considerable potential he had as a novelist at the beginning of his career. Unfortunately his schoolmasterly inclinations find a vent through Waymark, who sets out to educate each.

"My ideal woman is one who, knowing every darkest secret of life, keeps yet a pure mind—as you do, Ida," Waymark says (Ch. 14). He finds it difficult to suppress the temptation to indulge his passion for her. His attraction to Maud is expressed with a predictable difference: "Never was his blood so calm as in her presence. She was to him a spirit, and in the spirit he loved her" (Ch. 21). He oscillates between the two, weighing the prospect of marriage with each. Ida, if she proves worthy, would be offered simply a free union; but, by a curious logic, Maud would be offered marriage. "The necessity for legal marriage would be a confession of [Ida's] inferiority," he says, "and the sense of being thus bound would, he well knew, be the surest means of weakening his affection." On the other hand, "the thought of thus binding himself to Maud had nothing repulsive, for the links between them were not of the kind which easily yield, and loyalty to a higher and nobler nature may well be deemed a duty." He concludes, mystifyingly, "So far logical arguing" (Ch. 21).

Waymark merely seeks to rationalize old prejudices. He finally joins himself to Ida, who through heroic self-effacement grows in the end to be an idealized figure. When she becomes, as well, an heiress in her own right carrying out acts of benevolence among the poor, she regresses partly to the type of earlier philanthropic heroines. The rescue of the prostitute does end in a romance like the "New Arabian Nights";[25] but Gissing did something daring enough for his time in making her central to his novel, and suggesting at the same time the questionable moral worth of her foil, Maud Enderby, who retreats to the cloister. The novel as a whole highlights the unresolved problem of the split Victorian ideal of woman as either saint or prostitute.

The Unclassed appeared to herald the emergence of another English Realist besides George Moore to match French examples. Meredith advised Gissing to stick to the sphere defined in the novel, predicting "a foremost place for him in fiction" if he did.[26] It is tempting to speculate whether his achievement as a novelist might have been qualitatively greater if he had followed Meredith's advice. In the event, Gissing became more interested in the social changes brought about by the democratic process, and his novels developed greater affinities with the problem novel just coming into vogue. Especially in the nineties, Gissing's writing offered him a means of exposing the shoddiness which was invading English society.

While, as we have seen, Gissing did wish to see improvements in the general opportunities open to women, he proved to be adamant in his belief that the relations between the sexes needed no change. Any departure from the convention of lifelong marriage could not be justified on grounds of morality, or even of simple expediency. *Denzil Quarrier* (1892) is, in a fairly pure form, a novel with such a thesis. Gissing wanted to illustrate the truth of the proposition that an extramarital union brings personal disaster, and is therefore not desirable. The theme resembles that of Meredith's *One of Our Conquerors,* which appeared only the year previously, but the novels are otherwise quite dissimilar. An inclusive social imagination combined with energetic literary techniques gave Meredith's novel a depth and an originality absolving him of any attempt to impose his views upon the reader. Gissing, concerned with narrower issues, asserted firmly, "The book is, in fact, a strong defence of conventionality, and most people seem to understand that."[27]

Now, an extramarital union presents its partners with two major problems, as one might think: loss of social status owing to contravention of a legal rule and a social convention, and greatly increased difficulty in making psychological and emotional adjustments against the background of an earlier attachment sanctioned by law. Gissing chose to deal with the first—and lesser—problem, bypassing the more interesting challenge of the second. He appears to have wanted to enforce the traditionalist view that unless one partner dies, a serious sexual relationship cannot be superseded by another (or others) equally serious.

The extramarital union in *Denzil Quarrier,* although sympathetically presented, does not contradict this. Lilian Northway's marriage, contracted according to law, is in fact null and void. "She was a girl of seventeen, remember," Quarrier says,

> "... Well, the wedding-day came; they were married; and—just as they came out of the church, up walks a detective, claps his hand on Northway's shoulder, and arrests him for forgery. . . . He was sent to penal servitude for three years." (Ch. 9)

This clinically neat way of disposing of the first attachment is reinforced by making the husband, when at last he appears, a crude blackmailer. Quarrier meets Lilian while Northway is in prison and persuades her to live with him, though they keep their association secret. In reality, as we must say, there is only the one attachment to consider, that of Quarrier and Lilian, and only one problem involved, that of deciding whether it is just to enforce a marriage that has not gone beyond the church door, let alone been consummated. The novel amounts to no more than an elaborate exposition of this technicality; Quarrier's cry that he and Lilian are "face to face with the world's immoral morality" in having to hide their attachment (Ch. 9) sounds melodramatic and unconvincing. In the end, Lilian drowns herself through fear of prejudicing Quarrier's public life, and he exclaims, in the final sentence of the novel, "Now I understand the necessity for social law!" The bourgeois quality of Gissing's moralism is nowhere more evident than in this novel. The *Nation,* discussing it, observed,

> That English novelists now make no bones about the discussion of marriage versus *l'union libre* indicates a widespread modification of public opinion. The misery which they generally heap upon those who have preferred the illegal arrangement, or who have imagined themselves to be driven to it, may also be taken to indicate that they don't mean to hustle the British nation into any sort of anarchy which includes free love.[28]

Denzil Quarrier exposes unwittingly the chief artistic flaw in novels with theses. Presented centrally, the theses took precedence over the characters involved and thereby reversed a cardinal emphasis of fiction. The *Bookman,* commenting on this reversal of emphasis in Gissing's novel, pointed out that while the opening chapter leads us to expect "a study of results issuing from the characters of the unlawfully wedded—or unwedded—pair," the harmony between the pair remains perfect to the last, and thus "instead of a tragedy of character we have a tragedy of circumstance with a somewhat commonplace moral."[29] *Denzil Quarrier* was Gissing's first attempt at the short one-volume novel form.[30] The lack of the spaciousness to which he had been accustomed over a decade and his general unfamiliarity with the new restrictions of the form, together with the speed at which he wrote (*Denzil Quarrier* appeared only four months after it was begun), may have persuaded him that direct concentration upon his theme would present his meaning more economically. The straightforward public lecture by Quarrier entitled "Woman: Her Place in Modern Life" (Ch. 7), which echoes many of the author's own reservations on feminist issues, probably stemmed from the same search for economy.

Immediately after *Denzil Quarrier,* Gissing reverted to the three-volume form, bringing out *Born in Exile* in the same year (1892), *The Odd Women* in 1893, and *In the Year of Jubilee* in 1894. The latter two novels, projected simultaneously, resemble each other closely. In each he linked the discordant social reality around him with the feminist movement, and implied that liberationist ideas gave direct rise to the social vulgarity he detested. Each book, he declared, was to be "a study in vulgarism—that all but triumphant force of our time." He wanted "to deal with the great question of 'throwing pearls [that is, education] before swine,'" adding, pointedly, ". . . women will be the chief characters."[31] His presentation of the Madden sisters in The Odd Women is not completely the unambiguous expression of his sympathy for single women which it may be taken to be; they were also to symbolize the growing vulgarity of society. In the event, Gissing failed to achieve this second aim, but the attempt to associate vulgarity with the supposed intrinsic feebleness of female nature has undeniably left the spinsters, especially Alice and Virginia, more pitiably repellent than they need have been. The Spectator conceded that the individual studies might be true, but not the picture as a whole.[32] Never one to distance himself from his narrative, Gissing embraces too readily the idea of women's helplessness which he thought was due to the half-education they had received, and also to their secondary place in the scheme of things.

As for the career feminists whom he knew, Gissing could not resist distinguishing them from something called, at the time, "the womanly woman." In his novels they affect a mannishness of bearing, their countenances betray incipient masculinity. They are either guilty by innuendo, like Mrs. Wade who is partly blamed for Lilian's death in Denzil Quarrier; or under the tutelage of a typical Gissing hero they rather unconvincingly acknowledge the folly of their ways, like Rhoda Nunn in The Odd Women and Nancy Lord in In the Year of Jubilee.

Gissing tried hard to present Rhoda Nunn, the dedicated feminist in The Odd Women, in a fairer light than he had presented Mrs. Wade. Rhoda channels her animosity against men toward a constructive social ideal. She would train the women who will remain unmarried to lead useful and satisfying rather than futile lives. They would learn commercial skills like typing, but principally, they would be educated in self-respect and self-restraint to help them maintain their dignity in relations with males. Marriage in particular renders a woman vulnerable; rather than concede its necessity, the extreme feminist would abjure it, even anticipating a time when there would be a complete dissociation of the sexes. Rhoda says,

". . . before the female sex can be raised from its low level there will have to be a widespread revolt against sexual instinct. Christianity couldn't spread over the world without help of the ascetic ideal, and this great movement for woman's emancipation must also have its ascetics." (Ch. 6)

Cecilia Cullen in George Moore's *Muslin* and Olive Chancellor in Henry James's *The Bostonians,* expressing similar sentiments, are presented as neurotics. Gissing is determined to counter this doctrine through a rather blatant appeal to the "natural" order in love where man is the hunter and woman the prey. Barfoot, the ubiquitous Gissing hero of this novel, smugly tells Rhoda, "Love revives the barbarian. . . . Marriage by capture can't quite be done away with" (Ch. 17).

In the role of hunter Barfoot finally evokes a response of mixed curiosity and pleasure in Rhoda that passes in the novel for love. But he would have his subjugation of her more complete. He would test the strength of her convictions by proposing that they form a free union. Rhoda pleads for a legally sanctioned marriage. The relationship later falls through when an improbable coincidence arouses Rhoda's jealousy.

The *Academy* criticized Gissing's manipulation of this point. In another novelist's hands, it said, Rhoda would have "vindicated her fine character," but Gissing allows her to break down in the crisis.[33] She had deprecated marriage, but now it seems she has a secret preference for the old-fashioned marriage service. The *Academy* concluded, "One feels that Mr. Gissing has deliberately denied to her the success which she ought to have had." On both literary and polemical levels, an excellent opportunity was lost to illuminate love as a duel of the sexes, as August Strindberg had done in his play *The Father* only six years previously.

Gissing's efforts to relate feminist issues to a wider social background were crowned with a remarkable kind of success in *In the Year of Jubilee* (1894). The novel successfully climaxes his efforts to record imaginatively the rootlessness of the strange new class of people engendered by the spread of democratic opportunity through society. Written in rage, it strikingly confirms the view that Gissing wrote best about the "vulgarism" he hated so much. Sympathy for the predicament of women who remained unmarried had stayed his hand somewhat in his portrayal of the Madden sisters; he did at least commiserate with them in their fate. No trace of authorial partiality lightens the presentation of Fanny and Beatrice French and their married sister Ada Peachey in *In the Year of Jubilee*. Gissing drew the domestic anarchy of their household with relentless venom, and made their lives symptomatic of the qualitative loss taking place in society. Beatrice is stigmatized by trade, a word whose vulgar connotations in nineteenth-century society Gissing heartily endorsed. Gissing indicts her sister Fanny no less severely on the ground of her loose behavior. The characters of the French sisters hardly change throughout the novel. Gissing merely embellishes his personifications of indelicacy and commercial-mindedness each time they appear. Their incessant wrangling reaches a climax of uncouthness in Part 4, Chapters 4 and 5.

It is impossible to dismiss as merely fortuitous Gissing's association of the vulgarization of society with the changing character of women. The chaos of his own domestic life during his second marriage undoubtedly contributed to his authentic picture of brutishness among the half-educated. He abhorred imcomplete education because it left its recipients unaware of duties and responsibilities. No wonder the *Nation* said, "A not unfair generalisation from the novel would be that modern education and opportunity have demoralised women."[34] In a special way Gissing saw the sense of order in the community undermined by the opportunities now open to women. He was sympathetic with them in their desire for emancipation; he might even speak up theoretically in favor of "sexual anarchy" as a transitional stage toward more equitable relations between the sexes. But Gissing was too close to the stuff of life he dealt with. Confronted by domestic and moral turmoil, he recoiled with loathing from the tawdriness of the "emancipated" women whom he saw as the cause of it. "Wherever you look nowadays there's a sham and rottenness; but the most worthless creature living is one of these trashy, flashy girls," old Mr. Lord says,

> "the kind of girl you see everywhere, high and low,—calling themselves 'ladies,'—thinking themselves too good for any honest, womanly work. Town and country it's all the same. They're educated; oh yes, they're educated. What sort of wives do they make, with their education? What sort of mothers are they? Before long there'll be no such thing as a home. They don't know what the word means." (*In the Year of Jubilee*, Pt. 1 Ch. 5)

The chief male characters of *In the Year of Jubilee*, however else they may be differentiated, are of one and the same mind on the topic of the necessary subordination of women to men.

Through Nancy Lord, the heroine of *In the Year of Jubilee,* Gissing presented the positive side of his thesis about the necessarily subordinate role of women rather more compassionately, but still with firmness. The successful portrayal of this character strongly attests to the integrity of the author's continued efforts to understand the new role women sought to play in society. As with his other characters, Gissing ultimately rested his analysis of his heroine's character upon class displacement. She has acquired a spirit of independence at which Gissing looks askance. "Abundant privilege; no obligation. A reference of all things to her sovereign will and pleasure" (Pt. 2, Ch. 3)—the author conveys his view of her liberated state in such terms, and in their wake comes the author's inevitable suggestion of incipient masculinity. Through the story of her marriage, Gissing asserted that claims for the liberation of women must be limited by their role as mothers with a duty to bring up their children. A trite conclusion from one who had interested himself in women's problems over many years. Men are absolved from any significant revaluation of their own role. Women may read to improve their minds, but Gissing reaffirms the older view that woman's place is in the home.

There is nothing progressive, either, about the marriage experiment which Tarrant proposes to Nancy when he returns from America. "For such work as mine, I must live as though I were not married at all," he tells her (Pt. 6, Ch. 3). The arrangement might conceivably ensure the woman's greater independence as well, an idea which Grant Allen in the following year made the theme of his novel *The Woman Who Did.* In Gissing's use the theme is purely reactionary. Nancy is simply to keep house—and "read"—and care for their child; Tarrant, living separately, will visit her according to his inclination. The theory is that this will keep their love alive. That he might be unfaithful to her is a possibility he dismisses, invoking airily the double standard of morality: "Infidelity in a woman is much worse than in a man," he says. "If a man really suspects his wife, he must leave her, that's all; then let her justify herself if she can" (Pt. 6, Ch. 3).

Nancy does not flinch even when Tarrant—whom the *Saturday Review* termed, with some justification, "a combination of uninteresting loafer, cur and prig"[35]—tells her kindly, "True, I am your superior in force of mind and force of body. . . . We can't afford to disguise that truth" (Pt. 6, Ch. 3). Nancy accepts his teaching with marvelous docility saying,

"After all, one can put up with a great deal, if you feel you're obeying a law of Nature. Now, I have brains, and I should like to use them; but Nature says that's not so important as bringing up the little child to whom I have given life."

She fully understands the consequences of her attitude, and with the following speech she surrenders everything that women's liberationists had been fighting for:

"One thought that troubles me is, that every generation of women is sacrificed to the generation that follows; and of course that's why women are so inferior to men. But then again, Nature says that women are born *only* to be sacrificed. I always come round to that. I don't like it, but I am bound to believe it."

This cheerless conclusion, a reaffirmation of the "intention-of-nature" argument in biological terms, stands as practically the last explicit word by the author on the subject of women's claims to equality.

This last section of the novel, which Gissing converts to his didactic purposes, represents his final attempt to transplant liberationist issues into fiction virtually unchanged. If he was seeking a satisfactory form for the problem novel, he failed in this objective as well, since this final section (which includes the whole of Part 6) does not harmonize with the rest of his novel. Bertz had made this criticism, and Gissing assented in it.[36]

III

Gissing's novels of the nineties are curious hybrids, sustained on a literary level by his skill (discussed below) in older techniques of narrative and characterization. They invaluably supplement our knowledge of the social turbulence of the last decade of the nineteenth century. By keeping close to the refractory surface of ordinary lives, Gissing found his place in English fiction as the delineator of an emerging but still indeterminate class of society; and his loathing for its philistinism transformed the social historian into artist, despite his prejudices.

The marriage histories portrayed in these novels have a kind of seedy authenticity. Few could know better than Gissing the bitterness that could arise among maladjusted couples. One of his earliest successes with this theme was in *The Unclassed* (1884), where in the marriage of Julian Casti and Harriet Smales he produced a chilling though abbreviated picture of a sensitive man's mortification in a bond which nullified every normal human feeling. Here Gissing was also at the heart of perhaps the most intractable moral problem of the age: the seeming unsuitability of the traditional conception of marriage in an era where ideals and duties were changing rapidly.

Gissing presented the impasse in marriage again in *The Odd Women* in the story of Widdowson and his wife Monica, the third of the Madden sisters; in *In the Year of Jubilee* he showed how wide the gulf between husband and wife could be in his portrayal of the half-demented Ada Peachey and her husband Arthur. These marriages, forming important subplots, serve as the unamenable reality against which emancipationist theories were tested. No progressive theory could have much value which failed to alleviate this seemingly repetitive and harassing phenomenon. In his novels, Gissing brought these failed marriages into progressively closer contact with his feminist themes. His manner of doing it, however, reveals the limitations of his grasp of the issue of marital incompatibility. Largely influenced no doubt by his own harrowing experiences, he roundly blames the woman in each case for prejudicing the stability of the relationship. The men would be able to do the world's work, or pursue the ideal of secluded and cultured living, he seems to say, if only the women did not seek an exaggerated degree of independence in their lives.

Gissing's partiality for the male point of view was offset by the authenticity of his depressing histories, a quality which appreciably increased the literary merit of the novels. When in *The Whirlpool* (1897) Gissing at last dealt centrally and at three-volume length with a foundering marriage relationship, he had therefore devoted much thought to the problem and had the benefit of repeated preparation, as it were, for its literary presentation. *The Whirlpool* is Gissing's most skilful novel in every respect, but it has rarely been discussed. It embodies his mature vision with a technical assurance that must rank it very high among novels of the final decade of the nineteenth century.

In his delineation of the marriage of Alma Frothingham and Harvey Rolfe in *The Whirlpool,* Gissing at last mingled successfully his views on liberationist ideals with those on marriage. "The theme is the decay of domestic life among certain classes of people and much stress is laid upon the question of children," he wrote.[37] Originally he planned to

123

title his novel "Benedict's Household," which further confirms that he had given up interest in theoretical marriage experiments for their own sake. He told H. G. Wells that in the characterization of Rolfe, "I wished to present a man whose character developed with unusual slowness, and who would probably never have developed at all, after a certain stage, but for the change wrought in his views and sentiments by the fact of his becoming a father."[38]

The novelist had clearly subdued any trace of a desire to be merely polemical in his approach to the issues of the day, and now wished to make a mature examination of a basic responsibility. At first, Harvey Rolfe adopts the position of an opinionated male intellectual with assured means. "People talk much sentimental rubbish about children," he says, ". . . they're a burden, a hindrance, a perpetual source of worry and misery. Most wives are sacrificed to the next generation—an outrageous absurdity" (*The Whirlpool,* Bk. 1, Ch. 2). He is drawn gradually into the whirlpool of society; rather as Lydgate succumbed to Rosamond in George Eliot's *Middlemarch,* Rolfe slides into marriage with Alma Frothingham (Bk. 1, Ch. 11). His child awakens him to a sense of parental responsibility and to the general problem of educating children for a society which had lost much of its sense of tradition. It also brings him to a realization of limits that must be drawn to a woman's independence, since Alma, nervously wrapped in the pursuit of her musical career and in the social life accompanying it, leaves her domestic relationships to founder as they may, or uses them to further her own ambition.

As in *In the Year of Jubilee* and many of his previous novels, Gissing sought again to enforce a didactic conclusion: that a woman could not be fully emancipated without baffling her husband in his efforts to make their marriage successful. In *The Whirlpool* the author's point of view, while still remaining obvious, is woven with far greater skill into the novel's substance. Here, a reader may disagree with the view but would nevertheless concede that the novel's considerable worth is not thereby greatly affected. Gissing omitted author intrusions, and his strict dramatic presentation, interweaving narrative, feminist opinions, and character, proved to be highly effective. It is more fair to look for the summation of Gissing's views here than in his other novels.

His principals are well matched. Their marriage begins, for once, on terms of full equality, the fundamental demand of the feminist. But Alma's plans to embark on a career as concert violinist gradually estrange her from her husband, and their relationship thins steadily over two or three years into a tense and brittle cordiality. On the professional level, too, Alma progressively loses command over her power to make independent decisions, and fails to realize the vulnerability of her imagined freedom. In social circles she finds her self-respect set at nought. Felix Dymes, a hack composer and impresario, invites her to be his mistress. Cyrus Redgrave, the millionaire, patiently mines her path with subtle favors having the same objective. Alma herself soon becomes adept at using her admirers for her own purposes until the socialite Mrs. Strangeways, in reality Redgrave's go-between in his amours, places her in the compromising circumstance that leads to Redgrave's death. Alma retains just enough control over herself after this event to give a moderately successful recital, and then suffers a nervous breakdown. Events thereafter reveal the innumerable venalities she has committed at the expense of others to satisfy her own ego. Gissing's own accents are not far away in Rolfe's realization of how little his interests had mattered to her:

> Herein, of course, Harvey did but share the common lot of men married; he recognized the fact, and was too wise to complain of it even in his own mind. Yet it puzzled him a little, now and then, that a woman so intelligent as Alma should in this respect be simply on a level with the brainless multitude of her sex. (Bk. 3, Ch. 6)

Through Rolfe, Gissing reasserted his belief in the permanence of marriage as a fundamental social institution and in the incontrovertible superiority of men over women. Remarkably unoriginal conclusions after decades of moral tumult.

For all Gissing's skilful presentation of character, that of Alma Rolfe shows a bias against the independent woman impossible to ignore. Alma is a completely negative character. Where Rolfe is a scholar, she is a mediocrity not only in learning but even in her art; where he is generous and understanding, she is actuated by petty jealousies and unrelieved malice. Every setback that she suffers, each new act of compromise, serves for Gissing as a fresh item in an accumulating body of evidence illustrating her folly. To put it crudely, he gives her enough rope to hang herself, and she does. Gissing told an absorbing story but he sacrificed, unwittingly, any claim to expose Alma as representative of her sex.

It is worth recalling that contemporary criticism of Gissing's novels was far more stringent than ours today. He ruefully admitted that

"the public commonly speak of me as a 'woman-hater!' "[39] Gabrielle
Fleury, the one woman who brought him a measure of real happiness, evidently needed some reassuring on this score, and Gissing
was compelled to make a strenuous, revealing disclaimer: "Gabrielle,
once and for all let me tell you that I recognize no restraint whatever
upon a woman's intellect. Don't judge me in this respect from my
wretched *books*—which deal, you know, with a contemptible social
class for the most part."[40] But it was the books he was judged by.
The *Saturday Review,* in a critique of *The Whirlpool,* declared, "Our
women folk are not all angels, but . . . they are not invariably fools,
wantons, sneaks, and nagging sluts. Mr. Gissing's sustained snarl at
the sex at large grows a shade wearisome, not to say vexatious."[41]
However, the *Bookman*'s moderately argued reaction came much
closer to the point.

> While we acknowledge his fine care in the representation of
> [Alma], we feel that we are reading a conscientious school-
> master's report. Over and over again a more sympathetic inter-
> pretation occurs to one. For he is a pedant to human nature.
> Some temperaments when he touches them ring always false or
> sound flat. No novelist has taken more pains to understand the
> condition of the average woman's life today, to study her ambi-
> tions, to mete out to her an austere kind of justice. But the
> schoolmaster in him is ever deploring their methods. . . . And
> so the best of his women are not women at all, but illustrations
> out of a treatise on the times.[42]

The portrait of Alma Rolfe confirms also Gissing's ultimate
bafflement by the sex, his realization that for all his experience and
all his theories there existed a residual mystery about women which
he would never fathom. *Eve's Ransom* (1895), the one-volume novel
immediately preceding *The Whirlpool,* had anticipated this final position with both neatness and economy.

While *The Whirlpool*'s artistic merit makes it an extremely readable
novel, it is also something of a literary curiosity: a well-nigh perfect
Victorian three-decker appearing nearly twenty years after its vogue
had properly ended. It was in fact published as a single volume, but
its format in three "books" corresponds to the old three volumes.
The stuff of the plot consists, as did that of much earlier fiction, of
simple misunderstandings, for example, Alma's unfounded suspicion
that her husband has had a liaison with Mrs. Abbott, and culminates
in a somewhat melodramatic murder, that of Cyrus Redgrave. The

narrative, dispersed among a number of characters, proceeds at much the same deliberate pace which George Eliot had used to such advantage. Gissing did imitate her in many respects.[43] The study of the floundering marriage of Alma Frothingham and Harvey Rolfe, the author's central concern, does not differ much in kind from that of, say, Rosamond and Lydgate. The discrimination of motive in the characters resembles George Eliot's in its reliance upon a relatively unsophisticated psychology, but without her massive intelligence. Furthermore, some of the moral problems that Gissing deals with are defined by compromising circumstances—for instance, Alma alone in the house of the bachelor Redgrave—rather than by conflicting individual inclinations. We have only to think of *The Unclassed* to recall that at the outset of his career Gissing had tried to understand the latter type of problem, and it would seem that he found it insoluble for he never went back to it in the novels which followed. Finally, as in earlier fiction, while the evocation of milieu is detailed, the complex social interrelations themselves are again presented—in the symbol of the whirlpool—as inimical to human happiness.

Although Gissing's literary endeavors over seventeen years culminate rather ironically in a kind of throwback to an earlier type of novel in form, structure, and theme, his people nevertheless belong clearly to their own period with its tumult of expanding trade, social climbing, loss of group cohesion, and uncertain standards of sexual conduct. The early chapters capture vividly the sense of disintegration of English society into a meaningless whirl of barbaric influences. Gissing originally meant his novel to retain this scope throughout. Discussing its theme with Wells, he said, "I have come to recognize a course of things which formerly I could not—or would not—perceive; . . . I have a conviction that all I love and believe in is going to the devil; at the same time I try to watch with interest this process of destruction."[44] However, as his characters developed he was drawn, unwittingly, once again to his favorite presuppositions and, as the *Saturday Review* pointed out in the critique already referred to, forgot all about his original central purpose in writing the novel. In Frank Swinnerton's view, the novel "resembles rather the stirring of muddy waters than the authentic whirlpool which the author aims at presenting."[45]

The portrayal of women aside, the novel deservedly won both critical and popular success. H. G. Wells drew attention to its remarkable contemporaneity. The change taking place in Rolfe's mind, he wrote, is sweeping over the minds of thousands of educated men:

It is the discovery of the insufficiency of the cultivated life and its necessary insincerities; it is a return to the essential, to honourable struggle as the epic factor in life, to children as the matter of morality and the sanction of the securities of civilization.[46]

Wells believed *The Whirlpool* revealed the quality of a beginning—perhaps a rather thoughtless remark to make of one who had been writing for nearly twenty years. Ironically, it turned out to be the opposite: it was the novelist's utmost—and final—effort of artistry.

Gissing is the only novelist of stature to embody in his fiction the attitudes of reasoned opponents to women's freedom at the time when the movement had finally made its impact on the day-to-day living of ordinary young women. He is much more than the social historian William Plomer makes him out to be:[47] his bitterness over the social changes he witnessed and the integrity of his attempts to understand them lend to even his limitations a harsh vividness which still communicates itself to us today. At the same time he is rather less than a major novelist because his focus is too close to his subject-matter to permit a proportioned selection of detail or careful discrimination of essentials from ephemera. Strictly speaking his novels are problem-novels which, though far superior to the common run of examples in this subgenre, still did not achieve full artistic stature in the way the problem-play did in the hands of Ibsen. It is not necessary to award Gissing bad marks for being antifeminist per se. That, on balance, is what he was, and it would be patronizing to think the fact needs to be glossed over, especially since it was an integral part of his attitudes as a whole. There is no doubt that it gravely interfered with the novelist's selective process—even as uncritical partisanship of the opposite variety has now consigned numerous other novelists of the period to irretrievable anonymity. At least with Gissing, his perspective of wider social concern lifts him easily above the common rut. It is only when we examine the areas where this concern is attenuated by his residually *petit-bourgeois* presuppositions, including those relating to women, that we understand the peculiar place he occupies between major and minor novelists in the late nineteenth century.

6 Hardy: "The Fiction of Sex and the New Woman"

Contemporary readers did not hesitate to class *Jude the Obscure* (1895) as a problem-novel. The *Critic* referred to it as "an especially good specimen of a class of literature which has of late years come as a disturbing element into English fiction."[1] R. Y. Tyrell, too, agreed that in respect of the tone and scope of the book, "We cannot but class it with the fiction of Sex and the New Woman, so rife of late."[2] Some aspects of Hardy's novels are better understood in the context of the general development of the problem-novel, although not until *Jude the Obscure* did he take over completely the liberated heroine and her problems. Obviously, *Jude* is not simply a problem-novel, but it represents in important ways the climax of the development of this novel form so far as it evolved in England in the nineteenth century.

In the years immediately preceding *Jude the Obscure,* readers had been treated to a run of novels presenting heroines in varying degrees of emancipation animating their authors' views on the role of woman in society, the injustices women suffered in marriage, and the feasibility of free unions as a means of accommodating sexual relationships with greater fairness to both sexes and a higher prospect of permanency. Few, if any, of these novels are read today. Thematically and artistically, they covered little ground which the major novelists in this study did not deal with more effectively. The single-minded concentration on themes of women's liberation during these years answered a need of the time, and underlines a phase in English fiction during which writers believed in their power to influence society directly. "The struggle of ideas is commencing," wrote Henry Norman soon after Olive Schreiner's *The Story of an African Farm* appeared in 1883, "and the victorious ideas will demand prompt embodiment in our civilisation." He predicted that in the future the novelist would "guide, mediate, warn or destroy, as need shall be."[3] The minor problem-novelists seem to have had intentions as explicit as Norman had forecast, but rarely with the artistic power or the depth of understanding to support their endeavors.

In effect they explored the possibilities of a form of novel that promised to parallel developments which Ibsen had introduced into the drama. *A Doll's House* in translation made its impact on the English public and especially on progressive young women from 1880 on though it was not produced until 1889.[4] It was the literary equivalent of a manifesto for the New Woman. Olive Schreiner referred to the play as "a wonderful little work . . . [showing] some sides of woman's nature that are not often spoken of, and that some people do not believe exist."[5] Olive Schreiner and her friends formed a literary circle for reading Ibsen's plays and frequently such personalities as George Bernard Shaw and Edward Aveling participated in the readings. An Independent Theatre Association was also formed to sponsor the production of Ibsen's plays. Hardy was a founder-member, as were George Meredith and George Moore.[6] On the whole, the achievement of the Norwegian dramatist showed English novelists that the issue of the freedom of women could be treated polemically and still be great art.

Lyndall, the central character in *The Story of an African Farm*, heralded a series of liberated heroines disillusioned with the social conventions and the moral code of society, and determined to initiate fresh standards of conduct on behalf of their sex. The characterization of Lyndall carries more conviction, however, than those of most of her successors. Her independence and her spirit of defiance grow naturally out of her life on a remote African farm. On the whole, she avoids striking the attitude of the self-conscious reformer. Personal motives loom larger in her defiance of society than partisan ones, and make her character credible. The chapter in which she confides to her childhood friend her sense of a total social fabric inimical to the dignity of women catches quite successfully the somber passion of emancipationist discontent (Pt. 2, Ch. 4). Olive Schreiner's dialogue has a childlike intensity; combined with her dramatically cryptic narrative it gives an air of minor allegory, almost, to the trials of a young woman who would be free.

The skips and jumps in the author's narrative succeed only partially in shielding her inability to pursue her themes with vigor. While some of the long disquisitions are interesting in themselves, others frequently end in a species of obscurantism, as in Part 2, Chapter 1. Yet the themes of religious doubt and women's freedom, in growing uniquely out of a simple environment, achieve an unexpected and pleasing artistic validity. Olive Schreiner knew the life she described, and many episodes in her novel have the ring of autobiographical truth. Her heroine is courageously conceived and worthy of being remembered from the host of thinly sketched characters who followed in her wake.

The articulate heroine grew to be one of the most important features of the problem-novel, but many writers did not understand the artistic sources from which articulateness should spring. In the hands of too many, the characters became simply expository, lacking the genuine sense of either grievance or moral awareness which gave life to one like Lyndall. The short-story writer George Egerton was one of the few, apart from Olive Schreiner, to seek her inspiration in the realm of felt emotion. Her stories in *Keynotes* (1892) and *Discords* (1894) have been described as pioneering efforts in the modern short story. They catch her subjects often at the moment when they begin to realize the great resources of moral stamina necessary in forming human relationships, dissolving them, and forming new ones. Few minor writers appeared to realize that here was rich, permanently interesting material for the novelist. Many instead closely echoed the public arguments or mistakenly imbued their heroines with unnecessarily sentimentalized and glorified characters.

Most writers who dealt with the theme of free love held no brief for general promiscuity. Neither, as we have seen, did feminists on the whole aim at such a conclusion to their campaign. With the elimination of traditional forms and ceremonies, it was believed, lasting unions between men and women would be possible on the basis of love. However authors might expatiate on the theme of the free union, their heroines eventually came to see the error of their ways and consented afresh to adhere to the traditional forms. Nevertheless, ultimate recantation did not subdue the excitement of Victorian readers over the increasingly common use of a theme which only a decade previously would have been unthinkable in a novel. Besides Olive Schreiner and George Egerton, Grant Allen was probably the only other writer to refuse to accept this stock device of final recantation. His novel, *The Woman Who Did,* appearing in 1895, created the kind of sensation which indicated that the end of the vogue of the problem-novel was near. *The Woman Who Did* ran through at least twenty-one editions in the year of its publication, creating a furor exceeded only by Hardy's *Jude the Obscure.* According to Malcolm Elwin, "So many publishers refused the book that Allen was only deterred from destroying it when E. W.

B. Nicholson, realising its eventual curiosity as a revolutionary document, proposed to house the manuscript in the Bodleian."[7] Finally, Lane's decided to publish it. Its appearance served to intensify the attitudes of partisans on both sides on the subject of female emancipation. The heroine, Herminia Barton, refuses the "vile slavery" of marriage with the familiar fervor of the dedicated feminist. "To sell my kind for a mess of pottage!" she exclaims, ". . . I can't be untrue to my most sacred beliefs" (*The Woman Who Did,* Ch. 3).

Artistically, the book is an utter failure, surviving only on the grounds of historical interest and of the sensation it caused. D. F. Hannigan hailed it enthusiastically as "the Evangel of Free Love," and praised it for dealing with the relationship between the sexes "so thoroughly, so fearlessly, and, it might be added, so purely."[8] It is easier to agree with H. G. Wells who, while conceding that he sympathized with Grant Allen's ideas, declared that "this hasty, headlong, incompetent book seemed like treason to a great cause." Few novels of the period devolved so exclusively on the opinions and actions of a single character. In attacking the absurdly idealized characterization of Herminia Barton, Wells therefore criticized its fundamental weakness. "She seems to us to be a kind of plaster cast of 'Pure Womanhood' in a halo, with a soul of abstractions, a machine to carry out a purely sentimental principle to its logical conclusion."[9]

The Woman Who Did illustrates the species of literary self-stultification to which minor writers finally brought themselves. They went to absurd lengths to idealize their characters as a compensation for their advanced views, or as a persuasive device designed to make them more acceptable in new roles. Some writers may have been influenced in such efforts by George Eliot's great idealized portrait of Dorothea Brooke. There was, for example, the heroine of E. T. Papillon's novel *Alleyne* (1895), who marries in order to put her theories about woman's divine mission into practice. Her husband turns out to be an alcoholic and her marriage becomes a trial to her. Then a glance at a print of the Virgin in a shop window reminds her of her ideal of womanhood and gives her fresh purpose—"a kind of idealised Mariolatry," as the *Westminster Review* called it, illustrating the decay into which George Eliot's conception had fallen.[10]

Whatever the quality of the idealization, Hippolyta Valence (W. Barry, *The New Antigone,* 1888), Bertha Lancaster (Frank Frankfurt Moore, *"I Forbid the Banns,"* 1893), Herminia Barton, and many other heroines resemble one another in amounting to little more than the sum of a number of opinions on the injustices women suffered in society or on the attractiveness of unions sanctioned by love rather than social forms; and nearly all these views, except when fleetingly transformed by an Olive Schreiner or a George Egerton, drearily echo the pros and cons of emancipationist issues. Rarely in the history of the English novel had opinions and attitudes rendered such service in lieu of art on behalf of a contemporary movement. Still these journeymen, in keeping the issue alive on the social scene, undoubtedly influenced Gissing and Hardy to attempt to bring it closer to the novel's art.

For all their frankness in dealing with possible alternatives to conventional marriage, the most striking mark of the failure of the problem-novelists is that few of them took any real account of individual sexual or psychological motivation, an omission which amounted to a fundamental falsification since, after all, the free sexual union was their theme. In spite of the superfine insistence by their heroines on unions sanctioned by love alone, it was often a form of permanent marriage which these heroines envisaged, and not, as their views partly implied, a relationship which could be made and broken repeatedly, according to the fluctuations of desire. This was a reality the problem-novelists, in general, did not face. They concerned themselves chiefly with prophesying an ideal for the future—much as George Eliot had done—and results showed that, in the absence of tremendous creative energy such as George Eliot's, the novel was unable to support such a function exclusively. It remained for Hardy, long preoccupied with the theme of sexuality in human behavior, to give these minor novelists an object lesson in their field.

I

Participating in a symposium entitled "The Tree of Knowledge" in 1894, Hardy questioned "whether civilisation can escape the humiliating indictment that . . . it has never succeeded in creating that homely thing, a satisfactory scheme for the conjunction of the sexes."[11] Hardy did not consider that the difficulty of justifying marriage as a lifelong bond arose simply from the inequalities suffered by women. Here he differed in major respects from campaigning feminists. His novels do illustrate everywhere specific legal, social, and sexual injustices suffered by women, similar to those highlighted in John Stuart Mill's *The Subjection of Women.* Many of these injustices serve as subsidiary detail enhancing the contemporary flavor of his works. For example, after Troy's disappearance, Bathsheba finds herself in a minor legal plight vis-à-vis her tenancy of the Upper Farm mainly because of difficulties stemming from her status as a woman (*Far From the Madding Crowd,* Ch. 48); Thomasin Yeobright (*The Return of the Native*) and Grace Melbury (*The Woodlanders*) endure their husbands' escapades, for the most part with the decorous restraint of well-brought-up young ladies; Michael Henchard actually sells his wife Susan for five guineas in an odd episode at the outset of his extraordinary career.

Hardy's treatment of such instances confirms his sympathy with, and his understanding of, issues involved in the movement for female emancipation. Women often had the worse part to bear in marriage, and he showed this with increasing explicitness in every new novel. However, he did not consider that "the question of matrimonial divergence" could be resolved fully by simply restoring women to equal status with men.[12] Instead, he saw the irrepressibility of sexual feelings in both men and women as the crucial impediment to successful marriage. When asked in the symposium entitled "The Tree of Knowledge" to give his opinion on the topic of sex education for young women, Hardy recommended that "a plain handbook on natural processes be placed in the daughter's hands"; but he pointedly added, "Innocent youths should, I think, also receive the same instruction; for (if I may say a word out of my part) it has never struck me that the spider is invariably male and the fly invariably female."

As a writer Hardy insisted on the need for candor in dealing with matters of sex. In another symposium, he wrote, "Life being a physiological fact, its honest portrayal must be largely concerned with, for one thing, the relations of the sexes, and the substitution for . . . [happy endings], of catastrophes based upon the sexual relationship as it is."[13] The tragedy of sexuality lay in its waywardness, its unpredictability: desire cooled easily, and men and women sought new objects of pleasure because sexual passion ruled them far more strongly than was acknowledged. In Hardy's view, the unreason of sexuality, the inability of men and women either to keep instinct at bay or to order it along preconceived paths, undermined the Victorian ideal of marriage as an indissoluble tie, and produced the chief conflicts and disasters besetting mortal clay. This theme appears in as early a novel as *Far From the Madding Crowd,* and persists through

The Return of the Native to *The Woodlanders* and *Tess of the D'Urbervilles,* until in *Jude the Obscure* it receives final violent explication.

Hardy originally won fame as a writer in his role as storyteller. From a practical point of view, he had found it in his interests "to give up any points which may be desirable in a story when read as a whole, for the sake of others which shall please those who read it in numbers."[14] We may fairly conclude that the points he was ready to give up were social issues which might offend his readers. Writing thus to Leslie Stephen who, as editor of the *Cornhill Magazine,* which was serializing *Far From the Madding Crowd,* had no inhibitions about stating exactly what he required, Hardy added that while he hoped to have higher aims in the future, "for the present circumstances lead me to wish merely to be considered a good hand at a serial."

We need not regard this wish as wholesale capitulation; as a budding writer Hardy sensibly preferred to have his novels published rather than remain unpublished, and the Victorian reading public, he knew, was not yet ready to face the reality of sexual issues. For most of his career as a novelist, Hardy continued, though with increasing cynicism, to make alterations to his novels as editors and publishers demanded. These sacrifices, together with his undoubted ability in his chosen sphere, won him a capital advantage over his fellow-novelists: he enjoyed the confidence and respect of a wide readership and he could bring them around at their own pace to face the problems of "sexual mischance" which directly questioned the validity of contemporary social norms and institutions.[15] When the tempo of the feminist debate on sexual matters reached a peak in the nineties, Hardy, by then famous, felt accordingly released from editorial fetters, and presented his readers, in *Jude the Obscure,* with an uninhibited exposition of their sexual dilemmas.

Hardy's proven readiness to bowdlerize his novels at his publisher's request and the extremes to which he showed himself capable of going in his last novel *Jude the Obscure* encourage us to suspect the presence of sexual themes in even the early novels. Leslie Stephen, who once admitted to Hardy that "Remember the country parson's daughters" was the dire commandment he lived under as editor, turned down *The Return of the Native* while Hardy was writing it, because he feared "that the relations between Eustacia, Wildeve, and Thomasin might develop into something 'dangerous' for a family magazine."[16] Even when it was finally published, as J. W. Beach has pointed out, Hardy obscured the meaning of certain passages which confirmed beyond doubt the fact that Eustacia had been Wildeve's mistress before her marriage to Clym.[17]

Not till the collected works appeared in 1895 was Hardy able to restore these crucial instances to a fuller significance. Eustacia explicitly admits the fact of her sexual experience when, in summoning Wildeve to Rainbarrow, she says,

> "I have had no word with you since you—chose [Thomasin], and walked about with her, and deserted me entirely, as if I had never been yours body and soul so irretrievably!" (Bk. 1, Ch. 6)

But in the serial version this had been rendered comparatively innocuous by omitting the phrase "body and soul so irretrievably."[18] A few speeches later she decides to break off the liaison, saying,

> "You may come again to Rainbarrow if you like, but you won't see me; and you may call, but I shall not listen; and you may tempt me, but I won't give myself to you any more." (Bk. 1, Ch. 6)

In this instance, Hardy had to bowdlerize "won't give myself to" so that it read "encourage" in the serial version.[19] However, Wildeve exerts sexual power over one who has herself a predilection in the same direction. "To be loved to madness—such was her great desire. Love was to her the one cordial which could drive away the eating loneliness of her days" (Bk. 5, Ch. 7).

Eustacia's misgivings on the verge of flight with Wildeve (after Clym's denunciation of her for her culpability in the death of his mother) indicate a woman governed by a power of emotion which even he can hardly satisfy:

> "Can I go, can I go?" she moaned. "He's not *great* enough for me to give myself to—he does not suffice for my desire! . . . If he had been a Saul or a Bonaparte—ah! But to break my marriage vow for him—it is too poor a luxury!" (Bk. 5, Ch. 6, author's italics)

Hardy abbreviated this for the serial version in the following manner:

> "I can't go, I can't go! . . . No money: I can't go!"[20]

Hardy conceived Eustacia in unmistakably voluptuous terms. "She had the passions and instincts . . . which make not quite a model woman" (Bk. 1, Ch. 7). In his portrait of her in the famous "Queen of Night" chapter, the author devoted a good deal of attention to adding details that would suggest a woman tantalizingly capable of stirring men's sexual desires. Eustacia's mouth, for example, "seemed formed less to speak than to quiver, less to quiver than to kiss. Some might have added, less to kiss than to curl." In the general scheme of the novel, Hardy appears to have sought a compromise between, on the one hand, allaying suspicions that he altogether condoned Eustacia's frankly sensual nature, and sweeping the reader to sympathy for his erring heroine, on the other. Perhaps in order to make Eustacia's sexual propensities acceptable to ordinary readers, Hardy hinted that her nature had affiliations with evil, occult forces. Village gossip had it that she was a witch, and Susan Nunsuch went to the extent of pricking her with a long stocking-needle "to put an end to the bewitching of Susan's children" (Bk. 3, Ch. 2). Eustacia herself admits to a witchlike predilection when she lures Wildeve away from Thomasin, whom he is engaged to marry. "I merely lit that fire," she says,

> "because I was dull, and thought I would get a little excitement by calling you up and triumphing over you as the Witch of Endor called up Samuel. I determined you should come; and you have come! I have shown my power."

John Paterson's study of the successive revisions of this novel confirm that Eustacia was originally intended to suggest a satanic creature.[21]

To this complex of creative intentions, Hardy added an idealization of Eustacia's personality in a manner which answered to the tendency of the time to venerate woman as a goddess. "Eustacia was the raw material of a divinity," the author tells us. The aura of Comtean woman-worship suffuses his detailed presentation of her: "In a dim light, and with a slight rearrangement of her hair, her general figure might have stood for that of either of the higher female deities" (Bk. 1, Ch. 7). The rhetorical idealization of Eustacia, especially in the chapter entitled "Queen of Night," cannot be explained entirely as a tactical device designed to assuage his readers' sensibilities; Hardy was himself obviously attached to the ideal of woman as goddess, as George Eliot had been, too. In important ways Eustacia Vye also springs from the same kind of inspiration as Dorothea Brooke, who, we remember, was presented as a kind of latter-day Virgin Mary. Yet the contrast of these two figures indicates clearly the way in which the revaluation of the nature of woman was tending. In specifically marking Eustacia's sexual nature, Hardy deliberately sought to bring the mid-Victorian ideal of woman to earth; he revealed the goddess's mortal coils. "How I have tried and tried to be a splendid woman, and how destiny has been against me!" Eustacia cries (Bk. 5, Ch. 7). Within the limits permitted him by magazine fiction, Hardy implied that feminine destiny was closely associated with fleshly instincts. Thus when we go back to the numerous passages of *The Return of the Native* composed in a rhetoric influenced by the art of painting, we discover unsuspected irony.[22] The idealized portrait of Eustacia, beautiful as it is, is frozen in art. When she steps down from her pedestal she embraces contradictoriness. Hardy may have demolished this myth with too great an indulgence. There are considerable difficulties in discovering precisely how goddess, witch, and ordinarily sensual woman are related in the character of Eustacia. While she represents the author's first concerted effort to deal frankly with changing concepts relating to women, the novel itself is the product of conflicting artistic intentions.

Hardy antedates, by some thirty years, D. H. Lawrence's uncompromising attempts to define man and woman in terms of their responsiveness to sexual experience. It is true that Lawrence read much of his own profundity into Hardy's heroines, and that he read Hardy's novels often as if they were prototypes of his own. His "Study of Thomas Hardy," therefore, illuminates his own work more than it does Hardy's.[23] Yet Lawrence's corroboration that Eustacia represents "the primeval Female principle" suggests that even at the outset of the turmoil into which Victorian sexual ethics were thrown, Hardy instinctively chose the right tack. Unlike Lawrence, Hardy never fully escaped the strongly persistent Victorian notion of sexuality as intrinsically base and despicable, unhappily coarsening to feminine nature. However, even simply as a serial writer, Hardy's integrity did not permit him to ignore his new awareness of a fundamental motivation in human beings.

In *Tess of the D'Urbervilles* (1891), Hardy brought the creative intentions behind the portrait of Eustacia to a successful climax. Tess is a sexually attractive heroine who was also sexually motivated while retaining persuasively romantic coloring. Her presence is sung no more in terms of "Bourbon roses, rubies, and tropical midnights" as Eustacia's was. She is an epitome of womanliness described in passages full of sensuous imagery. Never again will the Victorian heroine be classed as a minor goddess. When we take into account the progress in the restoration of the original version of the novel traced by W. R. Rutland, it is clear that the question at issue was the degree to which it could be admitted in fiction that a woman consciously participated in—consented to—her own seduction.[24] While there is room for speculation about the precise degree of Tess's volition in the matter, the nature of the emendations virtually eliminates the possibility of her having been the object of unqualified rape. Much of the controversy around the novel devolved upon this issue. Tess was classed as either "a little harlot," or a "poor wronged innocent."[25]

Hardy's great art carried him through. By integrating Tess with her background organically, he created a memorable heroine. What Tess is in social terms is crucial in the consideration of the moral problem she raised. (By contrast, what Eustacia is in social terms counts for very little.) Tiller in the fields, harvester, dairymaid— Hardy's success in depicting these marks of Tess's social status as living, definitive stigmata of her personality made her come attractively alive for his readers, and compelled them, while pondering her social vulnerability, to commiserate at least with her strongly instinctual response to life.[26] But at a more general level, too, *Tess of the D'Urbervilles* represents a supreme effort on Hardy's part to represent sexuality as a general principle suffusing all life, an intention which adds particular piquancy to the rural fecundity of Tess's environment, especially during her idyllic sojourn at Talbothays. The soporific aura of neo-Keatsian sensuousness renders the conventional moral sense null. Tess and Clare feel they are in another Eden experiencing the benignancy of nature before the Fall (Ch. 20). Love counsels them "to snatch ripe pleasure" while the opportunity lasts, and they succumb:

> The "appetite for joy" which pervades all creation, that tremendous force which sways humanity to its purpose, as the tide sways the helpless weed, was not to be controlled by vague lucubrations over the social rubric. (Ch. 30)

Hardy's natural imagery differs strikingly from Meredith's, whose beautiful symbols mask more than they reveal the reality of sexual meaning. Hardy, less equivocal, anticipates D. H. Lawrence's treatment of sexuality as a function of universal growth and change, but Lawrence's complete and thoroughgoing perspective eludes Hardy. He probably did not fully seek consistency; the wintry environment at Flintcombe-Ash Farm, where nature in another and fatal mood gradually depresses his heroine, shows that he preferred to employ natural imagery for more diverse purposes (Ch. 43). Nevertheless, his partial vision probably influenced Lawrence and it contributes further to an explanation of the younger novelist's interest in his achievement.

The idyll in the Froom Valley has therefore some of the romantic seclusion of a remote Eden. Its sexual overtones are cocooned successfully from the rest of the novel so as to stand in immutable tragic contrast with the Victorian moral law. Further, so intimately did Hardy make his definition of chastity depend upon Tess's personality and upon the particular world in which she lived that its meaning for the sex as a whole is muted. Primarily, Tess is indeed the wronged maid of the ballad world, as Ian Gregor points out.[27] It appears as if a special plea is entered for a rather splendid exception. *Tess* comes close to a complete artistic resolution of a major spiritual dilemma, but the belief that nature does not fully accord with human wishes and human conceptions of love and happiness prevents it from bursting entirely its Victorian bonds.

In such ways Hardy's novels reflect directly the slow and difficult progress of the conventional Victorian psyche toward self-realization in matters of sex. He resigned himself to presenting his sexually errant characters as culprits whom society would have no hesitation in condemning. As he himself ironically said, he assumed for the purposes of his story that his readers would have "no doubt of the depravity of the erratic heart who feels some second person to be better suited to his or her tastes than the one with whom he has contracted to live."[28] In *Far From the Madding Crowd,* Sergeant Troy vacillates between Fanny Robin and Bathsheba, having a child by one, marrying the other. Marriage does not still Troy; he pursues his swashbuckling career until Farmer Boldwood, brooding with sexual desire for Bathsheba, shoots him for his irresponsible conduct. Fanny Robin, an early representation of the kind of camp follower whose misfortunes Josephine Butler's campaign did so much to publicize, dies in the simple manner of the wronged maid of the ballads. Leslie Stephen had especially insisted that her seduction be treated in a "gingerly fashion."[29] Both Eustacia and Wildeve vacillate in their affections, too; their plan to flee from their respective marriages could, according to the literary convention Hardy accepted, be met only with death: they are both drowned. Tess, for whom Hardy created a memorable world, meets death by hanging for submitting twice in extremity to Alec D'Urberville. D'Urberville, himself completely the creature of his sexual impulses, is stabbed. Jude's fevered history of passion ends when he dies of consumption. All who yield to their sensual natures are punished with death.

The question was not really of sexual excess. Hardy's protagonists could succumb to desire once, and their lives would fall ever after in the shadow of that first lapse. By contrast, his "good" characters—Gabriel Oak, Thomasin Yeobright, Grace Melbury, Giles Winterborne—evince hardly a spark of sexual feeling, a factor that probably explains, in Hardy at any rate, their relative colorlessness. In part, Hardy intended his numerous "murders" as a sop to upholders of the existing ethic. By killing off a character, he achieved a technically primitive but summary kind of poetic justice meant to assuage sensibilities outraged by the character's sexual waywardness.

But the method served at the same time as a stock device for generating sympathy for the character. Readers could move away from the dogmatic condemnation of sexual indulgence as axiomatically evil. They could perceive the incompleteness of moral judgments which classed his erratic characters as delinquents pure and simple. He did not propose any major alterations in the existing moral and ethical structure. His guilty protagonists were exactly that—guilty; he did plead that they be treated with compassion and understanding. But however we try to explain his readiness to accommodate his readers, there can be no doubt that his motive strongly affected his art. D. H. Lawrence put it strongly when he asserted, "Nothing in his work is so pitiable as his clumsy efforts to push events into line with his theory of being, and to make calamity fall on those who represent the principle of Love. He does it exceedingly badly, and owing to this effort his form is execrable in the extreme."[30]

II

By the time *Tess of the D'Urbervilles* appeared the problem-novel had established an undeniable vogue. Hardy had never shared the enthusiasm of its proponents for advancing solutions for the moral confusion of his contemporaries, but we have seen that he had cast about for some years for the best method of dealing with the issues which interested them. *Jude the Obscure,* too, was first projected in 1887, and Hardy has recorded the fact that Sue Bridehead was "a type of woman which has always had an attraction for me" although "the difficulty of drawing the type" had delayed his attempt to portray her.[31] When the novel finally appeared no one was left in any doubt that it constituted for its author "a new literary departure, amounting in effect to a desertion of the story of character in favour of the problem-novel."[32] The novel challenged its readers to recognize that no true adjustment between the sexes could be achieved unless it came to terms with the real nature of the bond between men and women which decades of complacency had done much to shroud. At the same time, through Sue's history, emancipationists and the minor problem-novelists were given their sharpest reminder of the complexities of human relationships which, in their fervor for a more equitable moral code, they had underestimated.

More clearly than in Tess's seduction, Hardy depicted the degree of passionate consent on Jude's part in his seduction by Arabella. After their separation Jude has hopes that his studies in Divinity will help him overcome his "animal passion" (Pt. 2, Ch. 3). But he is similarly stirred by Sue Bridehead, whom he meets not long after. He patiently panders to the changeability in her nature. She loves him but marries another, then returns to him but still will not consummate their relationship. A woman's independence of spirit, a worthy ideal in itself, has grown into a form of tyranny equal to any that men on their part may have devised. Jude's tragic history stems not only from his own sensuality, but also from Sue's obsessive concern for her own emancipated condition. He is left out on a limb after she renounces her independence and re-embraces convention in returning to Phillotson. As Hardy commented in a letter, her superfine insistence on sexual independence only "tended to keep [Jude's] passion as hot at the end as at the beginning, and helps to break his heart."[33] Sue herself admits, "It was damnably selfish to torture you as I did." Jude's resolution crumbles and, ironically, makes him Arabella's victim a second time, much as Tess succumbed twice to D'Urberville. The knowledge that Sue still loves him though she has returned to her lawful husband makes him reckless of his health and he dies.

The struggle of the Victorian heroine in late nineteenth-century fiction for liberation from her traditional role and personality comes to a climax in Sue Bridehead. Feminists of the time probably did not expect such a personification of their ideal. At last a novel had appeared which forcibly held up the mirror to their aspirations, which compelled them to face some of the major truths of the revolution in personality which they desired. Had Hardy's career as a novelist ended with *Tess of the D'Urbervilles,* his gallery of women would have been incomplete. The triumph of characterization which Tess represented

knowing

does not obscure the fact that she lived and moved chiefly on an emotional, not a cognitive level. She revealed no hint of intellectual restlessness; one may even say quite simply that she had no inner intellectual life. She exerted little or no choice over her fate; her responses did not stem from any interior dialectic of the mind. Sue, Hardy's only real intellectual heroine, fills a gap not only in the author's own book but in the history of the period as well. Her opinions, attitudes, and reactions combine to make her the best artistic representation of one of the most influential character ideals of the age. In weaving the theme of sexuality into her history and Jude's, Hardy revealed the moral confusion entailed not by feminist theories themselves but by the process of their application to actual life among people who did not fully comprehend them. Robert B. Heilman, in a recent essay which greatly increases our understanding of *Jude the Obscure,* has written a penetrating critique of Sue as "the true ultimate coquette."[34] It is worthwhile indicating specifically the connection between the coquetry and nineteenth-century radical emancipationism.

Sue possesses and faces the full consequences of the complete self-knowledge and independence of spirit for which a generation of New Women had striven. Her burning desire to be free asserts itself as sexual independence. She would retain at all times her right to deny sexual relations to her lover. Any number of improvements in woman's status without this fundamental right leaves her dignity in jeopardy by allowing, as Havelock Ellis called it, "the farmyard view of life to prevail," that is, one in which "the hen has no choice of her own."[35] Sue personifies the extreme refinement of sexual sensibility, the extreme moral fastidiousness, toward which idealizing young feminists unwittingly tended. One of Sue's reasons for fearing the marriage ceremony, Hardy explained in a letter, "is that she fears that it would be breaking faith with Jude to withhold herself at pleasure, or altogether, after it; though while uncontracted she feels at liberty to yield as seldom as she chooses."[36] Sue equates love with the fluctuations of desire and inclination: these impulses alone must sanction the sexual embrace; without either, a woman prostituted herself and sacrificed her essential independence.

A deep-seated neurosis results from the intensity with which Sue clings to this attitude. She denies that she is "cold-natured—sexless—on account of it" (Pt. 3, Ch. 4), but the fact remains that even before the story begins her attitude has driven to his death an undergraduate with whom she has lived. Throughout most of the novel, although she is genuinely attached to Jude, she holds him at a pitch of sexual desire in a similar fashion because of her ideal. Sue's neurosis has a wider significance: she does not merely defy law and convention, she has put herself so far beyond them in spirit in the pursuit of individual independence that her personality has become grievously impoverished. The shock administered to her by the grotesque deaths of her children reminds her suddenly of this impoverishment and of the immense distance she has put between herself and traditional values. In the end she marries Phillotson, and though from bitter experience of her moods he would be content with the form alone, she asks with gritted teeth for his conjugal embrace as well. The intensity and extremism of her emancipated outlook proves self-defeating: she returns the more fervently to the traditional fold.

Hardy admitted that the marriages repeatedly made and broken by Sue, Arabella, Jude, and Phillotson formed "a sort of quadrille."[37] Modern readers may not fully appreciate the significance of these constant matings and mismatings if they miss the novel's relevance in an emancipationist context. Albert J. Guerard says with some justification that Sue is "one of the most impressive in all fiction of a neurotic and sexually maladjusted woman—a living portrait rather than a case study, but with a case study's minute responsibility."[38] Nevertheless Hardy's heroine is essentially a pre-Freudian study; and the key to understanding both her neurosis and sexual maladjustment lies in her radical emancipationist idealism.

In *Jude the Obscure* the author presented with a hard precision some of the new truths which had emerged about the relationship between sexual desire, women's liberation, and social convention. Women's demands for independence ultimately involved a major revision of the concept of family, a process which would inevitably impose the maximum emotional and psychological strain upon both men and women. Eventually, women would exert a sexual tyranny equally detrimental to themselves and to men. Sue's sexual odyssey would have been hardly credible without her intellectualism. Only a woman with a high degree of intelligence could have gone through— and interpreted, oftener than not, rightly—the traumas Hardy saw as inevitable in the fully emancipated woman. This aspect of her characterization is oversolemn, pretentious, and a trifle ludicrous, as when she gives an account of her reading in Part 3, Chapter 4:

> "I have had advantages. I don't know Latin and Greek, though I know the grammars of those tongues. But I know most of the

Greek and Latin classics through translations, and other books, too. I read Lemprière, Catullus, Martial, Juvenal, Lucian, Beaumont and Fletcher, Boccaccio, Scarron, De Brantôme, Sterne, De Foe, Smollett, Fielding, Shakespeare, the Bible, and other such."

Hardy was employing the convention of the articulate, intellectual heroine established by the problem-novelists, and confirmed by Meredith's *Diana of the Crossways*. But the truest evidence of Sue's intellect rests on her fastidious moral sense, her fearless admissions of doubt, and her efforts to evaluate the social and moral significance of the role she sought in life.

The novel shares, then, some of the weaknesses of the problem-novel as a form. Its protagonists explain themselves relentlessly. They have little faculty for the small change of conversation; their predominantly expository function obstructs the complete realization of their artistic vitality. Yet they have a vividness, principally by virtue of their passions but also because they exist in a social and natural environment which Hardy drew with practiced skill and conviction. He was not entirely successful in his device—that is what it amounts to—for reminding Sue of the traditional bedrock in her personality. The episode of the child corpses underlined rather summarily how children had on the whole been left out of the debate on female emancipation. The deaths certainly numb Sue (and revolt the reader) without, however, losing their excessively contrived air. In Havelock Ellis's words, the episode constitutes the author's "one serious lapse."[39]

Jude the Obscure and Grant Allen's *The Woman Who Did*, both of which appeared in 1895, brought about the final daunting attack on the "New Woman" both in actual life and in the polemical fiction she had inspired.[40] Mrs. M. O. W. Oliphant saw "a crusade against marriage now officially organised and raging round us." She referred bitingly to the heroines of the new fiction as "these remorseless ministers of destiny, these determined operators, managing all the machinery of life so as to secure their own way." Hugh Stutfield began with a quip: modern fiction was "erotic, neurotic, and Tommyrotic." He went on to attack the "New Woman" as "a victim of the universal passion for learning and 'culture,' . . . full of 'ologies and 'isms, with sex-problems and heredity, and other gleanings from the surgery and the lecture-room." The fiction itself was described as "the fiction of erotomania," and simply "the charnel-house school."

The literary question of the moment was the place of sex in fiction. According to James Ashcroft Noble, *Jane Eyre* and *Adam Bede* exemplified the extent to which truth and boldness in dealing with matters of sex were both admissible and sufficient. By going beyond such standards, writers had created "the novel of redundant sexuality." His objection was that it was "ludicrously inartistic" to present men and women "as merely or mainly conduits of sexual emotion." Hugh Stutfield found "the prating of passion, animalism, 'the natural workings of sex,' and so forth," nauseating, and traced the development to the influence of the "French decadents." It was left to Mrs. B. A. Crackanthorpe to reiterate the dualistic approach of the Victorians to life in general, with renewed eloquence:

> We are part of nature, we are in nature, and by nature. But this natural world of ours is essentially dual; it is a body animated by a soul. . . . The two elements, the Real and the Ideal, must, if they are to produce a perfect harmony, have allotted to them equal rights and equal powers, for each is the necessary complement of the other. Explore, dissect, analyse the Real as the modern artist in letters may, there will be no new birth, no breath of life, for any of his brain-creations until the quickening spirit of the Ideal shall move upon the face of the waters.

Although feminists thenceforth lost the initiative in the field of literature as they had done in political affairs, there was no doubt that "the hundred-years'-end social-problematical novel" had made its mark. *Jude the Obscure* had brought the English novel to a point from which it could never regress. When Arabella threw the pig's genitals at Jude, English fiction as a whole received a crude phallic reminder symbolizing the aspect of human experience which novelists had to venture into if the novel itself was to continue to develop. In striving to come to terms with the sexual nature of men and women, Hardy rescued English fiction to a large extent from both provinciality and priggishness, and foreshadowed D. H. Lawrence's seminal treatment of the subject in the next generation.

The literary problem is how to relate evidence of women's social problems +cultural to the art of writing
↓problems 1. Yes their is a problem
2. How is problem deals in Novel if it is to be an art form?

Epilogue

One cannot avoid remarking in general that the leaders of the current women's liberation movement often depend on literary works to substantiate their expositions of the status of women in society. One of the aims of the present study has been to show that this resort to literature to identify facets of the general culture relating to women's problems should not be surprising. Present-day theorists have concentrated by and large on authors of the twentieth century, although some, like Germaine Greer in *The Female Eunuch* (1970), have made illuminating references to works from as far back as medieval times. Kate Millett has a small section of her book *Sexual Politics* (1969) on scattered individual works by Victorian writers (pp. 127-157 especially), and more substantial chapters on twentieth-century authors Lawrence, Miller, Mailer, and Genêt.

Greer, Millett, and others show clearly how literary works can be treated as documents offering evidence relating to particular social and cultural problems. What is less clear is whether these authors are sufficiently aware of the kind of literary problem faced in this book—that of relating the evidence to the art. There is a need for both kinds of approach, to be sure, provided we are aware of the distinction between them. The power of Millett's book, which uneasily straddles this distinction, rests on the starkness of her evidence, which leaves little remaining doubt about the nature of male chauvinism in sexual relations between men and women. Millett's provocative analysis of Lawrence's fiction may be regarded as the first though not the last word on the subject. The fineness of his art makes Ursula and Gudrun Brangwen more liberated than their predecessors, and develops the entire emotion of love to comprehensive realms which deserve more careful examination. Lawrence's complexity includes much more than the supremacy of male over female, but Millett's assault on the bias of his vision usefully reminds us to beware of the prejudices from which even visionaries are not exempt. In this respect, a more detailed and extended study of Lawrence's art—its structure and its style—can offer a genuine ad-

147

vance in our understanding of a much discussed literary figure. We should ascertain whether the distinctiveness of his art and his place in the tradition depend on his having introduced into modern literature "the truthful explicitness of pornography . . . [and] its anti-social character as well" (Millett, p. 46) rather more than on the health-giving philosophy of sex for which he has long been admired. In either case, a major revaluation of his work, taking modern liberationist views into account, would be worthwhile.

There is a point of crucial interest here. Did the battle for frankness in late-nineteenth-century fiction serve only to set the modern novel "off course"? Did frankness about what *is* become the criterion of good art at the expense of compassionate interpretations of all parties in human relations? The ideology of women's liberation in the nineteenth century, more than any other issue, encouraged the novel to seek to function in its truest sphere, which Graham Hough has described as "the sphere of human conduct, particularly conduct in its social relations" (*Image and Experience,* 1960, p. 208). Millett's driving analyses of Lawrence and other important twentieth-century authors show that these writers have missed Meredith's point about love being "an affair of two," and that there is no democracy unless the democratic process applies also to women. Meredith was the first modern formulater of a theory of sexual politics. But we have had to wait for Miller and Mailer to have the labyrinths of Willoughby's penetralia illuminated. The ghastliness of the spectacle has been one of the prime motivating factors behind the latest liberationist revival.

But where are the novelists to continue Meredith's good influence, Hardy's evenhandedness? How is equality to be restored in literature as well as in real life in our more baleful age? The liberationists are weakest in answering the latter question, although they sensibly avoid drawing up detailed utopian blueprints for the future. Equality is not similarity. This point, which George Eliot clarified with a combination of good instinct and analysis, continues to cause befuddlement. Some feminists mistakenly base claims for equality on similarity, even seeming to consider it necessary to prove first that they are human beings like men. As might be expected, they draw their evidence from advances in our knowledge about chromosome composition in our genetic makeup. But the argument from chemistry, however learned it can become, serves only to deflect us from the moral point of the equality of all. The chief problem still remains that of distinguishing functioning from conditioning, or as some authorities like Robert Stoller would put it, "sex" from "gender."

EPILOGUE

On the thorough conditioning to which women are subject, Germaine Greer's erudite book is an eloquent and authoritative testament. Greer fully vindicates the original insights of the creators of Lucy Deane and Rosamond Vincy, Olive Barton and Mildred Lawson, and Maud Enderby and the Madden sisters, about the character molds into which women are forced. At the same time, Millett's discussion of her authors has confirmed that their strenuous efforts to make love completely congruent with sex—sadistic sex at that—have brought to a point of exhaustion (I am aware of the pun) the "Don Juan" strain in modern Western fiction, the narrative of the hero in a picaresque search for boundless sexual experience. The evidence, in modern literature, of a triumphant viciousness in masculine sexuality has understandably stung many who appear to want to repay men in kind. As a result, radical feminism of the sort espoused by George Moore's Cecilia Cullen and Henry James's Olive Chancellor is now much more common: there will be no more marriage, men will be denied knowledge of the paternity of their own children, patriarchal society is to be swept away. The emergence of a doctrinaire hard line is balanced by the resilient intellectualism of more thoughtful writers who have established the justice of their cause. But if the women's movement today is to succeed in bringing about the reorientation of fundamental sexual attitudes which it desires, both halves of humanity must be involved, not just women.

A new breed of outstanding novelists (men and women) can, with our more numerous uncertainties about a true basis for sexual ethics, create the kind of context which enables a society to bring about change. Creative illumination is necessary, not just political argument and political action. One notes that hardly anyone has said anything about love—an admittedly vacuous concept at present. There may be a way to make it respectable—and central—once again. In her chapter on "Womanpower," Greer suggests that the exclusion of women from equal participation in all spheres of life in the past may have enabled them to retain "their power to perceive in henids" (p. 107), that is, the power to apprehend things through thought and emotion used together (where men valued more the power of intellect alone). Greer thereby revives, apparently without being aware of it, George Eliot's key concept of "emotional intellect." A hundred years after it was formulated as a faculty common to both sexes, this idea might yet prove to be the best means of dealing with the democratic quintessence in the idea of women's liberation, in actual life as well as in imaginative literature.

Notes

Chapter 1

1. The following would be important in any selected list: William Acton, *Prostitution, Considered in Its Moral, Social, and Sanitary Aspects* (London, 1857); W. Lyon Blease, *The Emancipation of English Women* (London, 1910); Josephine Butler, ed., *Woman's Work and Women's Culture* (London, 1869); Élie Halévy, *A History of the English People in the Nineteenth Century,* Epilogue II (translated by E. I. Watkin; London, 1934); Walter E. Houghton, *The Victorian Frame of Mind 1830–1870* (New Haven, 1957); Josephine Kamm, *Rapiers and Battleaxes: The Women's Movement and Its Aftermath* (London, 1966); Marian Ramelson, *The Petticoat Rebellion* (London, 1967); Sheila Rowbotham, *Hidden from History: 300 Years of Women's Oppression and the Fight Against It* (London, 1973); Theodore Stanton, ed., *The Woman Question in Europe* (London, 1884); Ray Strachey, *The Cause* (London, 1928); Ray Strachey, ed., *Our Freedom and Its Results* (London, 1936); Patricia Thomson, *The Victorian Heroine* (Oxford, 1956).

2. T. H. Huxley, "Emancipation—Black and White," *Collected Essays* (London, 1905), III, 66.

3. Mrs. Lynn Linton, "The Wild Women as Politicians," *Nineteenth Century,* 30 (1891), 79–88.

4. Auguste Comte, *A General View of Positivism,* trans. J. H. Bridges (London, 1865), p. 276.

5. Butler, *Woman's Work,* pp. 15–21 (author's italics).

6. John Stuart Mill, *The Subjection of Women* (1869, ed. Stanton Coit; London, 1906), p. 113. Citations of Mill's views are from this edition.

7. Statistics cited in Halévy, *A History of the English People,* pp. 492–497.

8. *Women's Suffrage Journal,* 1 September 1885, p. 139.

9. *Women's Suffrage Journal,* 1 January 1884, p. 2, reprinted the complete music sheet.

10. *Women's Suffrage Journal,* 1 September 1885, p. 139.

11. Stanton, *The Woman Question,* p. 5.

12. Strachey, *The Cause,* p. 189.

13. Butler, *Woman's Work,* pp. xvi–xvii (author's italics).

14. Alison Neilans, "Changes in Sex Morality," in *Our Freedom and Its Results,* ed. Ray Strachey, pp. 175–201 especially.

15. Blease, *The Emancipation of English Women,* p. 155.

16. Strachey, *Our Freedom and Its Results,* p. 181.

17. Butler, *Woman's Work,* p. xi.

18. See William C. Frierson, "The English Controversy over Realism in Fiction 1885–1895," *PMLA,* 43 (1928), 533–550. On the relation of Victorian pornography to the Victorian novel, see Steven Marcus, *The Other Victorians* (London, 1964), pp. 103–111.

19. See Clarence R. Decker, "Zola's Literary Reputation in England," *PMLA,* 49 (1934), 1140–1153.

20. Halévy, *A History of the English People,* Epilogue II, p. 484.

21. Mill, *The Subjection of Women,* p. 20n.

22. Karl Pearson, *The Ethic of Freethought* (London, 1888), Chs. 13 and 14. Citations of Pearson's views are from this work.

23. G. R. Drysdale, *The Elements of Social Science, or Physical, Sexual and Natural Religion* (1854; 7th ed. London, 1867), p. 4. Citations of Drysdale's views are from this work.

24. S. C. Cronwright-Schreiner, ed., *Letters of Olive Schreiner 1876–1920* (London, 1924), p. 129. Letter dated 26 January 1888. Abbreviated hereafter as *Schreiner Letters.*

25. *Schreiner Letters,* p. 151. Letter written in 1889 (author's italics).

26. *Schreiner Letters,* pp. 31–32. Letter dated 16 July 1884.

27. *Schreiner Letters,* p. 59. Letter dated 10 February 1885.

28. *Schreiner Letters,* pp. 151–152. Letter written in 1889.

29. See Mrs. Lynn Linton, "The Wild Women as Politicians," and "The Wild Women as Social Insurgents," *Nineteenth Century,* 1891, pp. 79–88, 596–605.

30. See "An Appeal against Female Suffrage," *Nineteenth Century,* 1889, pp. 781–788.

31. *Schreiner Letters,* pp. 198–199. Letter dated 6 November 1890 (author's italics).

32. See Lewis S. Feuer, "Marxian Tragedians," *Encounter,* 19 (November 1962), 23–32.

33. J. A. Banks and Olive Banks, *Feminism and Family Planning in Victorian England* (Liverpool, 1964), pp. 111–113.

34. See Peter Cominos, "Late Victorian Sexual Respectability and the Social System," *International Review of Social History,* 8 (1963), 23–27, 228–231.

35. *Schreiner Letters,* p. 217. Letter dated 10 January 1895 (author's italics).

36. Mona Caird, "A Defence of the So-called 'Wild Women,'" *Nineteenth Century,* 31 (1892), 811.

Chapter 2

1. Gordon Haight, *George Eliot: A Biography* (Oxford, 1968), p. 396.

2. *The George Eliot Letters,* ed. Gordon S. Haight, 7 vols. (Oxford, 1954–1956), II, 213–215. Abbreviated hereafter as *Letters.*

3. *George Eliot's Life as Related in Her Letters and Journals,* 3 vols. (London, 1885), III, 47. Abbreviated hereafter as *Life.*

4. *Quarterly Review,* 134 (January and April 1873), 366.

5. George Levine, "Determinism and Responsibility in the Works of George Eliot," *PMLA,* 77 (1963), 268–279.

6. Henry James, review of *Middlemarch,* reprinted in *The House of Fiction,* ed. Leon Edel (London, 1957), pp. 260–261.

7. In David Carroll, ed., *George Eliot: The Critical Heritage* (London, 1971); abbreviated hereafter as *The Critical Heritage.* Swinburne's review of *The Mill on the Floss* is reprinted at p. 163.

8. Unsigned review, *Westminster Review,* 74 (July 1860), 24–32, in *The Critical Heritage,* p. 142.

9. Unsigned review, *Spectator,* 33 (7 April 1860), 330–331, in *The Critical Heritage,* p. 113.

10. Unsigned review, *Saturday Review,* 9 (14 April 1860), 470–471, in *The Critical Heritage,* p. 116.

11. Ibid.

12. Joan Bennett, *George Eliot: Her Mind and Art* (Cambridge, 1962), p. 122. First published in 1948.

13. Charlotte Brontë, *Jane Eyre,* Ch. 27.

14. John Hagan, "A Reinterpretation of *The Mill on the Floss,*" *PMLA,* 87 (January 1972), 53–63.

15. A. C. Swinburne, *A Note on Charlotte Bronte* (1877), in *The Critical Heritage,* p. 165.

16. Unsigned review, *Saturday Review,* 9 (14 April 1860), 470–471, in *The Critical Heritage,* p. 118.

17. Dinah Mulock, unsigned review, *Macmillan's Magazine,* 3 (April 1861), 441–448, in *The Critical Heritage,* p. 157.

18. F. R. Leavis, *The Great Tradition* (London, 1955), p. 42.

19. Unsigned review, *Westminster Review,* 74 (July 1860), 24–32, in *The Critical Heritage,* p. 144.

20. *The Times,* 7 March 1873, pp. 3–4.

21. Barbara Hardy, *The Novels of George Eliot* (London, 1959), Ch. 3 especially.

22. *The House of Fiction,* p. 261.

23. W. J. Harvey, *The Art of George Eliot* (London, 1961), p. 154.

24. James F. Scott, "George Eliot, Positivism, and the Social Vision of *Middlemarch,*" *Victorian Studies,* 16 (1972), 59–76.

25. Martin J. Svaglic, "Religion in the Novels of George Eliot," *Journal of English and Germanic Philology,* 53 (1954), 148.

26. Barbara Hardy, *The Appropriate Form: An Essay on the Novel* (London, 1964), p. 109.

27. R. H. Hutton, review of *Middlemarch, British Quarterly Review,* 57 (1873), 407–429.

28. W. J. Harvey, "The Intellectual Background of the Novel: Casaubon and Lydgate," in *Middlemarch: Critical Approaches to the Novel,* ed. Barbara Hardy (London, 1967), pp. 25–37.

29. Hardy, *The Appropriate Form,* p. 121.

30. Harvey, *The Art of George Eliot,* p. 79.

31. George Eliot, *Impressions of Theophrastus Such* (London, 1879), p. 450.

32. Graham Martin, "*Daniel Deronda:* George Eliot and Political Change," in *Critical Essays on George Eliot,* ed. Barbara Hardy (London, 1970), p. 135.

33. *Spectator,* 45 (30 March 1872), 405.

34. R. E. Francillon, *Gentleman's Magazine,* 17 (October 1876), 411–427, in *The Critical Heritage,* p. 386.

35. On the general prevalence of equestrian imagery, see Hardy, *The Novels of George Eliot,* pp. 228–229.

36. John P. Kearney, "Time and Beauty in *Daniel Deronda:* 'Was she beautiful or not beautiful?,'" *Nineteenth Century Fiction,* 26 (1971), 290.

37. Hardy, *The Novels of George Eliot,* p. 227.

38. On the symbolism of reflecting glass, see Brian Swann, "Eyes in the Mirror: Symbolism in *Daniel Deronda,*" *Nineteenth Century Fiction,* 23 (1969), 434–445.

39. R. E. Francillon, *Gentleman's Magazine,* 17 (October 1876), 411–427, in *The Critical Heritage,* pp. 397–398.

40. Edward Dowden, *Contemporary Review,* 29 (February 1877), 348–369, in *The Critical Heritage,* p. 440.

42. R. R. Bowker, unsigned review, *International Review,* 4 (January 1877), 68–76, in *The Critical Heritage,* p. 435.

42. George Saintsbury, review of *Daniel Deronda, Academy,* 10 (9 September 1876), 253–254, in *The Critical Heritage,* p. 376.

43. Eliot, *Theophrastus Such,* p. 445.

Chapter 3

1. F. N. Lees, "George Meredith: Novelist," in *From Dickens to Hardy,* ed. Boris Ford (London, 1958).

2. *Letters of George Meredith,* 2 vols., ed. William Maxse Meredith (London, 1912), II, 412, 1 June 1888. Abbreviated hereafter as *Meredith Letters.*

3. *Meredith Letters,* II, 409, 16 March 1888.

4. *Athenaeum,* 1 November 1879, p. 555.

5. See Lionel Stevenson, *The Ordeal of George Meredith* (London, 1954), pp. 254–255.

6. For his long persuasive letter on this score see *Meredith Letters,* II, 529, 19 April 1902.

7. Reprinted in René Galland, *George Meredith and British Criticism* (Paris, 1923), review dated 14 April 1885.

8. *Meredith Letters,* II, 418, 2 November 1888.

9. *Meredith Letters,* II, 441, 3 November 1891.

10. *Meredith Letters,* II, 586, 1 November 1906.

11. *Meredith Letters,* II, 418, 2 November 1888.

12. See Irving H. Buchen, "The Egoists in *The Egoist:* the Sensualists and the Ascetics," *Nineteenth Century Fiction,* 19 (1964), 255–269. Dorothy Van Ghent also has some illuminating remarks on the same theme in her essay on *The Egoist* in her *The English Novel: Form and Function* (New York, 1961).

13. *Essay on Comedy,* p. 52.

14. *The Critical Writings of James Joyce* (London, 1959), p. 88; see also Donald Fanger, "Joyce and Meredith: A Question of Influence and Tradition," *Modern Fiction Studies,* 6 (Summer 1960), 125–130.

15. *Spectator,* 66 (30 May 1891), 763.

16. *Saturday Review,* 71 (23 May 1891), 626.

17. *Academy,* 13 June 1891, p. 555.

18. Quoted in Lionel Stevenson, *The Ordeal of George Meredith,* p. 290.

19. Among the exceptions is Jack Lindsay's *George Meredith: His Life and Work* (London, 1956).

20. *Meredith Letters,* III, 368, 5 June 1885.

Chapter 4

1. Joseph Hone, *The Life of George Moore* (London, 1936), p. 266. Abbreviated hereafter as Hone, *Life.*

2. George Moore, *Memoirs of My Dead Life* (1906), Ch. 1.

3. After *Confessions of a Young Man* (1886) and *Memoirs of My Dead Life* (1906) came the three volumes of *Hail and Farewell:* "Ave" (1911), "Salve" (1912), and "Vale" (1914), and *Avowals* (1919).

4. *Memoirs of My Dead Life,* Ch. 4, "The End of Marie Pellegrin," and *Confessions of a Young Man,* Ch. 20, respectively. The latter is clearly the source of his novel *Esther Waters* (1894).

5. *Confessions of a Young Man,* Ch. 14.

6. Preface to *Muslin* (London, 1932), p. x.

7. *Memoirs of My Dead Life,* Ch. 1.

8. *Avowals,* Ch. 10.

9. Angus Wilson, *Emile Zola* (London, 1952), p. 46.

10. Quoted in Hone, *Life,* pp. 93–94, 96.

11. *Muslin,* Preface.

12. *Confessions of a Young Man,* Ch. 17.

13. "The Case of *Esther Waters* (1894)," in Ian Gregor and Brian Nicholas, *The Moral and the Story* (London, 1962), p. 108. Helmut Gerber, one of the foremost Moore scholars at the present time, also refutes Nicholas' claim. See *George Moore in Transition: Letters to T. Fisher Unwin and Lena Milman 1894–1910,* edited with a commentary by Helmut Gerber (Detroit, 1968).

14. Walter D. Ferguson, *The Influence of Flaubert on George Moore* (Philadelphia, 1934), Ch. IV especially; C. Heywood, "Flaubert, Miss Braddon and George Moore," *Comparative Literature,* 12 (1960), 151–158; and Milton Chaikin, "George Moore's *A Mummer's Wife* and Zola," *Revue de Littérature Comparée,* 31 (1957), 85–88.

15. Henry James, *The House of Fiction,* ed. Leon Edel (London, 1962), p. 199.

16. Hone, *Life*, p. 101.

17. *Muslin*, Preface, pp. viii–ix.

17a. Martin Seymour-Smith, "Rediscovering George Moore," *Encounter*, 35, no. 6 (December 1970), 64, 65.

18. *Athenaeum*, 24 July 1886, p. 110.

19. Hone, *Life*, p. 187.

20. See, for example, the symposium on this topic in which fourteen well-known people (including Thomas Hardy, Sarah Grand, Israel Zangwill, and Walter Besant) took part: "The Tree of Knowledge," *New Review*, 10 (January-July 1894).

21. George Moore, *Celibates* (1895), "Mildred Lawson," Ch. 1.

22. *Yellow Book*, 7 (October 1895), 143.

23. Hone, *Life*, pp. 195–197; and "Lui et Elles" in *Memoirs*, 1921 edition only.

24. See William F. Blissett, "George Moore and Literary Wagnerism," *Comparative Literature*, 13 (1961), 52–71.

25. *Letters from George Moore to Edouard Dujardin 1886–1922* (New York, 1929), 28 September 1898. The subsequent quotations and bibliographical details in the rest of the paragraph have been drawn from Hone, *Life*, pp. 206, 214, 281, 283, 378; R. A. Gettmann, "George Moore's Revisions of *The Lake, The Wild Goose*, and *Esther Waters*," *PMLA*, 59 (1944), 540–555; the Carra Edition of Moore's works (New York: Boni and Liveright, 1924), which included three other novels not included in either the Uniform or the Ebury Edition, namely, *Lewis Seymour and Some Women, Spring Days*, and *Sister Teresa;* and Malcolm Elwin, *Old Gods Falling* (London, 1939), p. 101.

26. Enid Starkie, *From Gautier to Eliot* (London, 1960), pp. 35–36 especially.

27. Walter Pater, *Studies in the History of the Renaissance* (London, 1917), pp. 144–145.

28. Hone, *Life*, pp. 131–132.

29. George Moore, *A Communication to My Friends* (London, 1933), p. 78.

30. *Athenaeum*, 2 July 1898, pp. 31–32.

Chapter 5

1. Jacob Korg, *George Gissing: A Critical Biography* (Seattle, 1963), p. 185. Hereafter abbreviated Korg, *Gissing*.

2. Arthur C. Young, ed., *The Letters of George Gissing to Eduard Bertz 1887–1903* (London, 1961), p. 171, 2 June 1893. Hereafter abbreviated Young, ed., *Gissing to Bertz.*

3. George Orwell, "George Gissing," *London Magazine,* 7 (June 1960), 41.

4. Algernon and Ellen Gissing, eds., *Letters of George Gissing to Members of His Family* (London, 1927), p. 128, 18 July 1883. Hereafter abbreviated A. and E. Gissing, eds., *Gissing to Family.*

5. Korg, *Gissing,* p. 11.

6. R. A. Gettmann, ed., *George Gissing and H. G. Wells* (London, 1961), p. 264. Hereafter abbreviated Gettman, ed., *Gissing and Wells.*

7. Korg, *Gissing,* p. 13.

8. Young, ed., *Gissing to Bertz,* p. 112, 6 September 1890 (author's italics).

9. Young, ed., *Gissing to Bertz,* p. 110, 15 August 1890.

10. Morley Roberts, *The Private Life of Henry Maitland* (London, 1912), pp. 152–155.

11. George Gissing, *The House of Cobwebs and other Stories* (London, 1907), p. 257.

12. *Times Literary Supplement,* 28 December 1956, p. 780.

13. 21 December 1880 (Yale University Library), quoted in Korg, *Gissing,* p. 90. Similar views are expressed by the chief character in *Denzil Quarrier* (1892), Ch. 3.

14. Young, ed., *Gissing to Bertz,* p. 172, 2 June 1893.

15. Young, ed., *Gissing to Bertz,* pp. 151–152, 1 May 1892. See also A. and E. Gissing, eds., *Gissing to Family,* pp. 168–169, 22 September 1885; and p. 371, 8 July 1900.

16. Young, ed., *Gissing to Bertz,* p. 171, 2 June 1893.

17. A. and E. Gissing, eds., *Gissing to Family,* pp. 72–73, 30 May 1880 (author's italics). Again similar views are to be found in *Denzil Quarrier,* Ch. 7.

18. Young, ed., *Gissing to Bertz,* p. xxx.

19. Frank Swinnerton, *George Gissing* (London, 1912), p. 48.

20. George Gissing, *The Private Papers of Henry Ryecroft* (1903), "Spring," Ch. 16.

21. *Academy,* 28 June 1884, p. 454.

22. *Athenaeum,* 28 June 1884, pp. 820–821.

23. Korg, *Gissing,* p. 44.

24. A. and E. Gissing, eds., *Gissing to Family,* pp. 183–184, 31 July 1886.

25. "The Novel of Misery," *Quarterly Review,* 196 (October 1902), 400.

26. Mabel Donnelly, *George Gissing* (Cambridge, Mass., 1954), p. 84.

27. A. and E. Gissing, eds., *Gissing to Family,* p. 326, 14 March 1892.

28. *Nation,* 54 (28 April 1892), 327.

29. *Bookman,* March 1892, p. 215.

30. Young, ed., *Gissing to Bertz,* p. 137, 18 October 1891.

31. Young, ed., *Gissing to Bertz,* p. 144, 16 February 1892.

32. *Spectator,* 27 May 1893, p. 708.

33. *Academy,* 24 June 1893, p. 542.

34. *Nation,* 61 (17 October 1895), 277.

35. *Saturday Review,* 79 (19 January 1895), 100.

36. Young, ed., *Gissing to Bertz,* p. 193, 30 December 1894.

37. Young, ed., *Gissing to Bertz,* p. 219, 9 May 1896.

38. Gettman, ed., *Gissing and Wells,* p. 47, 7 August 1897.

39. Pierre Coustillas, ed., *Letters of George Gissing to Gabrielle Fleury* (New York, 1964), p. 42, 14 August 1898.

40. Coustillas, ed., *Gissing to Fleury,* p. 36, 8 August 1898 (author's italics).

41. *Saturday Review,* 83 (10 April 1897), 363.

42. *Bookman,* May 1897, pp. 38–39.

43. Korg, *Gissing,* pp. 259–260.

44. Gettman, ed., *Gissing and Wells,* p. 48, 7 August 1897.

45. Swinnerton, *George Gissing,* p. 112.

46. Gettman, ed., *Gissing and Wells,* p. 258, August 1897.

47. Introduction to the Watergate Classics edition of *In the Year of Jubilee* (London, 1947).

Chapter 6

1. *Critic,* 24 (28 December 1895), 437.

2. *Fortnightly Review,* January-June 1896, p. 858.

3. "Theories and Practice of Modern Fiction," *Fortnightly Review,* 1 December 1883, p. 886.

4. *Breaking a Butterfly*—a version of *A Doll's House*—was performed in 1884, "but was so altered and diluted that it could hardly

be called an Ibsen play" (C. R. Decker, "Zola's Literary Reputation and Victorian Taste," *Studies in Philology,* 32 [1932], 635).

5. *Schreiner Letters,* p. 14, 28 March 1884.

6. W. R. Rutland, *Thomas Hardy* (Oxford, 1938), p. 252. Abbreviated hereafter as Rutland, *Hardy.*

7. Malcolm Elwin, *Old Gods Falling* (London, 1939), p. 318.

8. D. F. Hannigan, "Sex in Fiction," *Westminster Review,* 143 (1895), 616–625.

9. H. G. Wells, *Experiment in Autobiography,* 2 vols. (London, 1934), II, 549–550.

10. *Westminster Review,* 143 (1895), 711.

11. "The Tree of Knowledge," *National Review,* 10 (1894), 681.

12. Preface (1895) to *The Woodlanders* (1887).

13. "Candour in English Fiction," *New Review,* 2 (1890), 15–21.

14. *The Life of Thomas Hardy 1840–1928,* compiled by Florence Emily Hardy (London, 1962), p. 100, ca. 1873. Abbreviated hereafter as Hardy, *Life.*

15. George Wing, *Hardy* (London, 1963), p. 11.

16. F. W. Maitland, *The Life and Letters of Leslie Stephen,* (London, 1906), p. 276.

17. J. W. Beach, "Bowdlerised Versions of Hardy," *PMLA,* 36 (1921), 634–640.

18. *Belgravia,* 34 (1877–1878), 499. (The serial version began in November 1877 and was completed in February 1879.) The same deletion occurred when the novel appeared as a book published by Smith, Elder and Co., in 1878 in three volumes (I, 135). Also noted in Beach, *PMLA,* 36 (1921), 637.

19. *Belgravia,* 34 (1877–1878), 501. The same deletion was made by Smith-Elder (I, 140–141). Also noted in Beach, *PMLA,* 36 (1921), 637–638.

20. *Belgravia,* 34 (1878–1879), 15. Smith-Elder made the same deletion (III, 200).

21. John Paterson, *The Making of the Return of the Native* (Los Angeles, 1960), pp. 17–30 especially.

22. See my essay, "Thomas Hardy's Rhetoric of Painting," *A Review of English Literature,* 6 (October 1965), 62–73.

23. The parts of this "Study" relevant to Hardy were reprinted in D. H. Lawrence, *Selected Literary Criticism,* ed. Anthony Beal (London, 1955), pp. 166–228.

24. Rutland, *Hardy,* pp. 223–227.

25. Hardy, *Life,* p. 245, 1892.

26. Arnold Kettle, *An Introduction to the English Novel,* II, Ch. 4.

27. Ian Gregor and Brian Nicholas, *The Moral and the Story,* (London, 1962), p. 141.

28. Preface (1895) to *The Woodlanders.*

29. Hardy, *Life,* p. 98.

30. D. H. Lawrence, *Selected Literary Criticism,* p. 189.

31. Preface to the first edition of 1895 of *Jude the Obscure;* Hardy, *Life,* p. 272, 20 November 1895.

32. Sir George Douglas, "On Some Critics of *Jude the Obscure,*" *Bookman,* 9 (January 1896), 120–122.

33. Hardy, *Life,* p. 272, 20 November 1895.

34. Robert B. Heilman, "Hardy's Sue Bridehead," *Nineteenth Century Fiction,* 20 (1966), 307–323.

35. Havelock Ellis, "Concerning *Jude the Obscure,*" *Savoy,* 6 (October 1896), 49.

36. Hardy, *Life,* p. 272, 20 November 1895.

37. Hardy, *Life,* p. 273, 4 January 1896.

38. Albert J. Guerard, *Thomas Hardy* (Oxford, 1949), p. 109.

39. *Savoy,* 6 (October 1896), 35–49.

40. The views quoted are drawn from the following selection: *Nation,* 62 (6 February 1896), 123; Mrs. M. O. W. Oliphant, "The Anti-Marriage League," *Blackwood's Magazine,* 159 (January 1896), 140; James Ashcroft Noble, "The Fiction of Sexuality," *Contemporary Review,* 67 (April 1895), 490–491; Hugh Stutfield, "Tommyrotics," *Blackwood's Magazine,* June 1895, p. 837; Mrs. B. A. Crackanthorpe, "Sex in Modern Literature," *Nineteenth Century,* 31 (1895), 614; D. F. Hannigan, "Sex in Fiction," *Westminster Review,* 143 (June 1895), 624–625; Blanche Leppington, "The Debrutalisation of Man," *Contemporary Review,* June 1895, p. 742.

Index

INDEX

Drysdale, G. R., 14, 17, 18, 19
Dualism. *See* Sex
Dujardin, Edouard, 101, 104

Education of women, general, 4,
    145–146
  in *MF*, 34
  in *M*, 44
  in *DD*, 53–54
  in Moore, 86–87
  in *EW*, 90–91
  in *MW*, 91–92
  in *DM*, 94–95
  in Gissing, 111–113
 in *OW*, 118
  in *YJ*, 119–122
  in *JO*, 145
  intellectual development, in Eliot,
    30
  in *MF*, 35–37
  in *DD*, 61–62
  in Meredith, 74
  in Moore, 85
  sex education, 15
  in "ML," *OC*, 99
  in Hardy, 133–134
  in James, 99
Egerton, George, 20, 21
  Keynotes, 131
  Discords, 131, 133
Eliot, George, 3, 12, 26–63, 82,
    133, 148, 149
  Adam Bede, 146
  Daniel Deronda, 12, 32, 33, 40,
    51–63
  Felix Holt, 26, 27
  Middlemarch, 3, 4, 12, 25, 32, 39–
    51, 53, 56, 62–63, 124, 127,
    132, 137, 149
  The Mill on the Floss, 32, 33–40,
    53, 62–63, 149
  Scenes of Clerical Life, 27
Ellis, Havelock, 19, 22
Equality/Similarity of men and
    women, biological, 148–149
  in Eliot, 28–33
  in *YJ*, 121–122
  intellectual, in *M*, 47–49
  in *DM*, 94

in Gissing, 107, 111–112
  in *TU, DQ, YJ*, 112–113
  in *TW*, 125
  legal, in Hardy, 13–14, 133
  moral, 2, 148, 149
  in Meredith, 74
  sexual, 15, 16, 18
  in Moore, 85
Evans, Isaac, 26
Extra-marital union, George Eliot
    and G. H. Lewes, 26–27
  in *DD*, 57–58
  in *OC*, 72–73
  in *MW*, 92
  in *DQ*, 116–117

Fawcett, Millicent Garrett, 6
Flaubert, Gustave, 96, 101
  L'Education Sentimentale, 91
  Madame Bovary, 86, 91
Fleury, Gabrielle, 113, 126
Francillon, R. E., 59
Free union, in Drysdale, 18
  of Eleanor Marx and Edward
    Aveling, 22
  of Gissing and Gabrielle Fleury,
    113, 126
  in *Keynotes* and *Discords*, 20–21
  in Pearson, 16
  in problem novels, 24, 131–133
  in *AF*, 20
  in *TU*, 115
  in *OW*, 119
  in *YJ*, 121–122
  in *JO*, 142, 143–144
French Realists/Naturalists, 10, 21,
    65, 84, 86, 88, 89, 91, 92–
    93, 106, 115
Function/Role of women, domestic
    theory, 2, 15, 21
  in *M*, 44–45, 48–49
  female principle in *RN*, 138
  "intention-of-nature" theory, 2, 3,
    21, 149
  in Eliot, 28–29, 40–41
  in *M*, 4
  in *TE*, 76
  in *DM* and *Doll's House*, 94–95
  in *YJ*, 121–122

INDEX

INDEX

INDEX